Jewish thought today

BY LOUIS JACOBS

Behrman House, Inc.

PUBLISHERS   NEW YORK

for Daniel

Published by Behrman House, Inc.,
1261 Broadway, New York, N.Y.

Library of Congress Catalog Card Number: 73-116679
Standard Book Number: 87441-014-2

Manufactured in the United States of America

International Standard Book Number: 0-87441-213-7

THE
CHAIN OF
TRADITION
SERIES

Volume III:
Jewish thought today

Illustrated by

Irwin Rosenhouse

THE
CHAIN OF
TRADITION
SERIES

Acknowledgment

With the appearance of the third volume of The Chain of Tradition
Series, my thanks are long overdue to Eugene B. Borowitz for his
skill in editing the manuscripts and his numerous valuable suggestions
for their improvement; and to Babette Schulman for a careful and close
reading of the text, and for bringing the volumes swiftly to completion.

The author and publishers wish to thank individuals and publishers
for their permission to use the copyrighted material contained in
this volume. Their names are included in the opening paragraph of
each chapter.

Introduction

FOR MORE THAN one hundred and fifty years Jewish thinkers have been concerned with understanding the role of Jews and Judaism in the modern world. This book contains the writings of some of these thinkers and by a careful reading of the selections presented here you will obtain a good idea of the new problems they had to deal with and the different ways they had of grappling with them.

Judaism in the past had been successful in coming to terms with various civilizations. The list of these is long—Babylonian, Egyptian, Canaanite, Assyrian, Persian, Greek, Roman, Christian, Islamic. It was impossible for Jews not to be influenced by the world around them, but they tried hard at the same time to remain true to their own faith. They tended to adopt the ways of the people among whom they resided when no basic Jewish principles were at stake, but to call a halt whenever there was a danger of accepting into Jewish life ways and ideas that would be harmful to the truth they had received by tradition.

Theoretically the problem of the Jew in the modern world was exactly the same as it had always been, but practically the situation was very different. For the first time Jews began to participate fully in the life of their neighbors and this to an extent unknown to previous ages. In the Western world, Jews became prominent among the philosophers, scientists, musicians, artists, lawyers, doctors, business-men and teachers. They made a decisive contribution to modern thought. For this reason it was no longer a question of the Jewish people as an entity facing a challenge from without. The many conflicts between the old and the new were present in the souls of most educated Jews.

The problems Jews have had to cope with in the modern world are of two kinds; those peculiar to Jews and those common to all religions. To the first kind belong such questions as how far should Jews allow themselves to become assimilated to the outside world? how much Hebrew should be retained in the Synagogue? what is a Jew to do if the only way he can make a living is to work on the Sabbath? are the dietary laws still binding upon Jews? what is the role of Jewish people-hood and, now, the State of Israel, in Jewish life? how can the Jew manage to be well informed about his own Jewish heritage if he has to spend so much time acquiring general culture and knowledge? As for the problems common to the adherents of other religions as well as the Jewish, these have to do with the breakdown of traditional theories on the nature of the universe. The earth is no longer seen as the center of the universe but the whole of our solar system is only a tiny speck in the vastnesses of space. From Darwin onward the view that man is descended from lower forms of life has won increasing acceptance. Marx and Freud questioned whether men are as rational as they like to imagine they are and have put forward the view that men are unconsciously motivated by social and economic forces (Marx) or by irrational strivings within themselves (Freud). The philoso-pher Kant in the eighteenth century questioned whether man can ever have any real knowledge of anything beyond his own world. The rise of modern science has encouraged men to look at their surroundings in terms of cause and effect so that, for example, the whole idea of God interrupting this sequence by performing miracles or in answer to prayer became more difficult to accept than in the earlier period Moreover the scientific methods of letting the facts speak for them-selves without preconceived notions were applied to the Biblical books and it was found, as a result, that many of the traditional posi-tions as to the date and authorship of these were no longer tenable.

Yet Judaism has displayed its astonishing power of survival. A number of movements arose, for example, which differed from one another in matters of emphasis, and even on fundamental principles, but all of which had the effect of paving the way for the necessary re-adjustment so that Judaism might survive and hold its own with renewed vigor.

The first of these movements was the *Haskalah* (Enlightenment), the aim of which was to prepare the Jew for his life in the new world by introducing him to its culture. The "enlightened" Jew was to be thoroughly familiar with the great classics of Western thought as well as with his own literature. Allied to this was the movement known as *Jüdische Wissenschaft* (The Science of Judaism). The aim of this school was to study the Jewish past in a scientific way, that is to say, to examine, so far as this is possible, not what we imagine to have happened in Jewish history but what actually did happen. At a later date Zionism arose. The Zionists taught that the Jews were a nation like other nations and could only flourish if they had a land of their own. Eventually, Zionism led to the establishment of the State of Israel. The bitter fact that six million Jews were murdered by Hitler gave a tremendous impetus to the search for a secure home for the Jewish people so that such terrible happenings might never occur again. In the State of Israel the Hebrew language is spoken, the Bible is widely read, and the whole of society is pervaded by the Jewish spirit, though this is not to say that all the problems are now solved; there are, indeed, new ones such as the role of religion in the new State and relations between Jews and Arabs.

On the religious level three new movements arose. Neo-Orthodoxy bravely faces up to the challenge of the new both by becoming thoroughly acquainted with modern life and thought and by denying that anything which has happened during the past one hundred and fifty years renders in any way the past insights out of date. Reform Judaism accepts the challenge in a different way. It holds that the heart of Judaism is to be found in the teachings of the great Hebrew prophets and these, which speak in God's name of justice, righteousness and mercy in daily life, are still as valid as ever. As for the ritual observances, Reform is prepared to see value in many of these but does not consider them to be of supreme importance. Conservative Judaism holds on to a mid-way position. It believes that Orthodoxy is too rigid in its resistance to change and Reform too ready to throw overboard cherished institutions such as the dietary laws and the traditional way of Sabbath observance. Consequently, it tries to follow the traditional pattern but with greater openness and a fuller appreciation of its dynamic quality.

The thinkers who appear in these pages belong to one or another of these movements. They do not represent, therefore, anything like a uniform viewpoint. If you find yourself agreeing with everything all of them say you will be guilty of indulging in loose thinking since they disagree profoundly among themselves. It is hoped, nonetheless, that this book will be acceptable to the adherents of all the different groupings because it does not seek to propagate any single viewpoint but prefers to let the various thinkers speak for themselves. Whatever your own attitude to these questions, you will come to understand it better by examining the views of its opponents. The thinkers are not labeled according to their movements. That should encourage you to examine their ideas without prejudice.

The book is divided into three parts. Part I deals with the way new thought on the Jewish doctrine of God serves to place the doctrine in the central position it has always occupied in Judaism but with a number of fresh insights into its meaning. Part II considers the doctrine of the Torah as the revealed will of God and how this can be understood in the light of our present-day knowledge. Part III treats the doctrine of Jewish peoplehood and its relevance for modern Jewish life. There are other problems with regard to Jewish life in the present but all the main ones have to do with these three areas. The notes to the various texts give some background information and try otherwise to elucidate the meaning of the texts. This is particularly important because some of these writers occasionally tend to assume a knowledge of Jewish thought which the average intelligent Jewish reader cannot be expected to possess.

It remains to be said that the following are *selections* from Jewish writers and thinkers and should be seen as a beginning or an introduction to the understanding of Judaism in the world of today. If they encourage the reader to go on to study these weighty questions in greater depth and detail the book will have achieved its purpose. For the rest practically every serious Jewish book published today is concerned with one or more of the problems discussed in these pages.

God

WITH FEW exceptions, the Jewish thinkers of the modern period follow more or less traditional views on the nature of God and His relationship to man. But Judaism teaches that God is manifested in the world and is to be approached through participation in the life of the world. It is obvious that the new views about the world and human life in it which emerged from the Renaissance onward were bound to have their effect on man's thinking about God. In particular, the scientific picture of the universe has compelled thinkers to re-evaluate religious beliefs. Some thinkers, Jewish and non-Jewish, were motivated by the dominant scientific view to think in more mechanistic terms, tending to look with great suspicion on such ideas as miracles and prayers of petition i.e., asking God to change the order of nature. Others tended to react to the scientific view by re-emphasizing the more personal aspects of religious life, believing that this is called for if man is to be seen as an individual created in God's image rather than a machine responding blindly to its environment.

Of the thinkers represented in this section Heschel is entirely traditional in his views though original in calling attention to our sense of wonder. The same applies to Leo Baeck, except that Baeck is rather

1

more modern in style and language, utilizing the idiom of twentieth century thought. Buber, more than any other thinker, stresses the personal aspect of God. His distinction between man's approach to things and his approach to persons is one of of the most fruitful religious ideas of our day. Mordecai Kaplan, on the other hand, is with the exception of Rubenstein, the most untraditional of the thinkers represented here, the one most influenced by the scientific picture. For Kaplan it is better to use terms like "Force" or "Power" when speaking of God, otherwise, there is, for him, the danger of thinking of God simply as a colossal human being, which is, of course, absurd. Rabbi Epstein is entirely traditional. Although he, too, uses the idiom of twentieth century thought, he, in fact, retains in its totality the medieval picture.

Many present-day religious thinkers hold that belief in God has to be taken on trust. It cannot be proved and reason has very little to do with it. Our selection on this theme is from the writings of Milton Steinberg, who is of the opinion that belief in God provides us, nonetheless, with the only reasonable account of human life and the universe as a whole. The most stubborn obstacle to faith is the horror of the Holocaust. Rubenstein accepts the critique, but Fackenheim shows how nonetheless faith is possible.

Epstein and Steinberg are fairly easy to follow. Kaplan, Heschel, Rubenstein and Fackenheim make rather heavier demands on concentration. Baeck and Buber, especially Buber, are very difficult and much effort is required to grasp their thought.

The way of reason

The reasonableness of belief in God.

Milton Steinberg (1903-1950), outstanding Rabbi, preacher and author, devoted a good deal of his short working life to examining the nature of the Jewish faith. The following selection is from the book compiled after Steinberg's death by Arthur A. Cohen, and contains Steinberg's essays on Judaism. The book is called Anatomy of Faith *(Harcourt, Brace & World, Inc., New York, 1960, pages 88-96). A few paragraphs have been omitted in order to give as much as possible of Steinberg's full argument within the scope of a few pages.*

Religion's world outlook centers about God. Before attempting to indicate what we mean by that word, let us first make clear what we do not mean. "God" does not denote an old man on a throne some-where up in the sky. That notion is in part a survival of the infancy of the human race, in part a hangover from our personal childhood, from those days when, having first heard about God and possessing only limited intellectual resources, we pictorialized Him according to our naïveté. However the conception is come by, it is far less innocent than is generally supposed. It impels many a person to regard himself as an atheist, simply because he does not believe that there really is an old man in the heavens. On the other hand, it condemns indivi-duals capable of ripe spirituality to the stuntedness, perhaps life-long, of puerile, unsatisfying, and undignified convictions.

The naive picture, says Steinberg, is not merely wrong but positively harmful because it distorts in a very childish way the greatest idea of all.

To believe in God, maturely, intelligently, is to believe that reality did not just "happen," that it is no accident, no pointless interplay of matter and energy. It is to insist rather that things, including man's life, make sense, that they add up to something. It is to hold that the universe, physical and moral, is a cosmos, not an anarchy . . . meaningful rather than mad, because it is the manifestation of a creating, sustaining, animating, design-lending Spirit, a Mind-will, or to use the oldest, most familiar and best word, a God.

The word "cosmos" is from the Greek and means the universe as an ordered whole. Hence Steinberg argues that the only way of seeing the universe as a cosmos rather than an anarchy is to see it as the product of a Mind which orders and this is God.

Here at last we come to the crux of our investigation. Are there any reasons for maintaining that the world is of this character rather than that, that Deity rather than Nullity moves behind and through it? There are such reasons, not one but a number, all good, indeed compelling.

God is the only tenable explanation for the universe. Here we are, creatures of a day, in the midst of a vast, awesome world. Sometimes it strikes us as a big, blooming tumult. But through the seeming confusion some traits persist, constant and all-pervading. Thus, the universe is *one,* an organic unity, subject everywhere to the same law, knitted together with interdependence.

Again, it is *dynamic,* pulsating with energy, movement, life. It is *creative,* forever calling new things into being, from stars and solar systems to new breeds of animals, new ideas in the minds of men, new pictures on the artist's canvas.

It is *rational* in the sense that everything in it behaves according to law! Electrons and protons according to the rules of their being, plants in harmony with their nature, animals after the patterns of their respective kinds, and man in consonance with the mandates not only of chemistry, physics, and biology but of psychology and the moral order as well. Everywhere: form, design, predictable recurrence, law.

The universe, furthermore, is *purposive;* at least it is in some of its phases. An insect laying its eggs in a place where the larvae yet to be born will be assured of food as they will require it; a spider weaving its web, a bird building a nest, an engineer designing a bridge, a young man charting his career, a government drawing up a policy, a prophet blueprinting a perfected mankind—all these are instances, rudimentary or advanced, conscious or instinctual, of planning ahead. Purposiveness is indisputably an aspect of reality, and no theory can be said to explain the latter if it does not account for the former as well.

The universe further contains *consciousness.* It has produced man. At least in him it discloses intelligence, a thirst for truth, sensitivity to beauty, a desire for goodness. And man is a component of reality. Whence it follows that no explanation of the entirety can be acceptable if it does not illumine the existence and nature of this most complex, challenging and mysterious of its components.

This then is the world in which we live: one, dynamic, creative, rational, and inclusive of elements of purpose, consciousness, and goodness. For such a universe the religious theory is by far the best "fit." Only *it* accounts at all adequately for the striking features just enumerated. That is why men of all eras, cultures, and capacities, including most of the world's great philosophers, have tended so generally to arrive, no matter what their point of departure, at some kind of God-faith. For, once one begins to reflect on the nature of things, this is the only plausible explanation for them.

Many thinkers have tried to prove the existence of God but many other thinkers, particularly in modern times, have argued that this cannot be done. Steinberg approaches the matter in a slightly different way. He asks us to consider which explanation of the world as we know it is better—that it is made by God or that it just happened. If this test is applied it becomes clear that the only explanation which fits the facts is the one that there is a God.

But what about the evil of the world? Can the God-idea account for *that?* Not entirely, and not to anyone's complete satisfaction. This fact unquestionably counts against faith. On the other hand, there are many interpretations of evil from the religious viewpoint whereby its existence can be reconciled, partially if not thoroughly, with the existence of God.

But even if evil were a total mystery on which theology could not make so much as a dent, the God-faith would still be indicated. For, at the worst, it leaves less unexplained than does its alternative. If the believer has his troubles with evil, the atheist has more and graver difficulties to contend with. Reality stumps him altogether, leaving him baffled not by one consideration but by many, from the existence of natural law through the instinctual cunning of the insect to the brain of the genius and heart of the prophet.

This then is the intellectual reason for believing in God: that, though this belief is not free from difficulties, it stands out, head and shoulders, as the best answer to the riddle of the universe.

Steinberg does not deny that the problem of evil is very difficult. But his point is that against this problem has to be set all the reasons for God-faith he has mentioned earlier. So that what it amounts to is this, the believer in God has one terrible difficulty but the atheist has a whole host of difficulties because he can offer no explanation at all for reality as we know it.

The second reason for belief in God is that man cannot live joyously, hopefully, healthily, perhaps not at all, without it. Consider what the universe and man look like under the assumption of atheism.

Reality appears totally devoid of point or purpose. Like everything else, man is seen as a by-product of a blind machine, his history a goalless eddy in an equally directionless whirlpool, his ideals random sparks thrown off by physiochemical reaction in the colloidal solution, compounded by chance, which is his brain. Everything adds up in the end to exactly nothing.

What is the consequence of such a view for man and society? Can it be other than discouragement, demoralization, despair? What else shall one say of it except that "that way madness lies."

And Steinberg goes on to say that, granted belief in God, man can, for all his troubles, find security in the knowledge that God is on his side in the fight against evil and He assures us that the good will eventually win out. He quotes the verse: "Fear not: for they that are with us are more than they that are with them" (II Kings 6:16).

But is this fair to atheists? Have not some of them been among the most unselfish and self-forgetting of mortals? And on the other hand, are not many of the most bestial and least idealistic of human beings religionists?

No, what we have just said, had it been said of atheists, would have been grossly unfair. But it does no injustice whatsoever to atheism, the inescapable effects of which are to trivialize ideals, to present the human enterprise as a futility, and so to undermine the classic ethic of justice, mercy, and self-negation on behalf of moral principle and human welfare.

But, if so, how is one to account for the goodness of so many irre-ligionists? Very simply. Men often behave better than their philosophy. Only they cannot be expected to persist in doing so. In the end, how a man thinks must affect how he acts; atheism must finally, if not in one generation then in several, remake the conduct of atheists in the light of its own logic.

Steinberg goes on to say that most atheists today are living by the morality originally taught by Judaism and through Judaism by Christianity and this morality stems from the Jewish belief in God. As someone has said, atheists who are moral are living on the spiritual capital stored up by their believing ancestors.

This statement of Steinberg is really a completely traditional approach to belief in God, though, naturally, he puts forward his argument in modern language and in terms of our present-day thought and experience.

The way of wonder

How man can come to belief in God.

Professor Abraham Joshua Heschel (b. 1907) is a leader of Jewish religious thought and a well-known spokesman for Judaism to the outside world. In the following Heschel describes the sense of wonder as basic to a sound religious outlook. The passage is from Heschel's book God in Search of Man *(Farrar, Straus and Giroux, Inc., New York, 1955, pages 45-50).*

Wonder or radical amazement is the chief characteristic of the religious man's attitude toward history and nature. One attitude is alien to his spirit: taking things for granted, regarding events as a natural course of things. To find an approximate cause of a phenomenon is no answer to his ultimate wonder. He knows that there are laws that regulate the course of natural processes; he is aware of the regularity and pattern of things. However, such knowledge fails to mitigate his sense of perpetual surprise at the fact that there are facts at all. Looking at the world he would say, "This is the Lord's doing; it is marvelous in our eyes" (Psalms 118:23).

Heschel argues that for all the explanations we have about how things work, man still finds within himself a sense of astonishment and wonder that anything is here at all. This marvelous world we see awakens us to the surprising fact that it is hard to believe it all just happened. With this realization man is led on to the idea that God must have created it all.

That "wonder is the feeling of a philosopher; and philosophy begins in wonder" was stated by Plato and maintained by Aristotle: "For it is owing to their wonder that men both now begin and at first began to philosophize." To this day, rational wonder is appreciated as *"semen scientiae,"* as the seed of knowledge, as something conducive, not indigenous to cognition. Wonder is the prelude to knowledge; it ceases, once the cause of a phenomenon is explained.

Heschel means that there would be no thinking at all without the sense of wonder. Because we are surprised at certain facts we are moved to investigate them. Thus wonder helps (is conducive to) cognition (thinking) but is not indigenous to it i.e. is not thinking itself. Heschel goes on to say that so far all philosophers agree, but that Heschel himself as a religious thinker attaches an even greater significance to the sense of wonder.

But does the worth of wonder merely consist in its being a stimulant to the acquisition of knowledge? Is wonder the same as curiosity? To the prophets wonder is *a form of thinking.* It is not the beginning of knowledge but an act that goes beyond knowledge; it does not come to an end when knowledge is acquired; it is an attitude that never ceases. There is no answer in the world to man's radical amazement.

The philosophers might say that while wonder is helpful as a stimulus to thought, eventually thought banishes wonder because once a thing has been explained reasonably there is no more cause for wonder. Electricity, for example, must have seemed very mysterious to the ancients but now that we know so much about it we have far less to wonder about. But Heschel still thinks that the fact of electricity is a very startling thing and that, indeed, the more we know about the properties of this world the more we are moved to wonder. When he says that there is no answer to man's radical amazement he means, of course, unless the answer is not found in the world at all but in God.

As civilization advances, the sense of wonder declines. Such decline is an alarming symptom of our state of mind. Mankind will not perish for want of information; but only for want of appreciation. The beginning of our happiness lies in the understanding that life without wonder is not worth living. What we lack is not a will to believe but a will to wonder.

Awareness of the divine begins with wonder. It is the result of what man does with his higher incomprehension. The greatest hindrance to such awareness is our adjustment to conventional notions, to mental clichés. Wonder or radical amazement, the state of maladjustment to words and notions, is therefore a prerequisite for an authentic awareness of that which is.

If we would see a sunset or a jet plane or the Empire State building for the first time we would certainly feel this sense of wonder. But we have become so accustomed to these and many other marvels that we become blasé and tend to feel that everything is really commonplace. "Maladjustment to words and notions" means that we must try not to become too adjusted to explanations of things and we must continue to marvel at the sheer wondrousness of things so that we are led on to the divine.

Radical amazement has a wider scope than any other act of man. While any act of perception or cognition has as its object a selected segment of reality, radical amazement refers to all of reality; not only to what we see, but also to the very act of seeing as well as to our own selves, to the selves that see and are amazed at their ability to see.

Radical amazement means the deepest kind of amazement of all, not that this or that particular thing is a source of wonder but that it is wondrous that there is anything at all.

The grandeur or mystery of being is not a particular puzzle to the mind, as, for example, the cause of volcanic eruptions. We do not have to go to the end of reasoning to encounter it. Grandeur or mystery is something with which we are confronted everywhere and at all times. Even the very act of thinking baffles our thinking, just as every intelligible fact is, by virtue of its being a fact, drunk with baffling aloofness. Does not mystery reign within reasoning, within perception, within explanation? Where is the self-understanding that could unfurl the marvel of our own thinking, that could explain the grace of our emptying the concrete with charms of abstraction? What formula could explain and solve the enigma of the very fact of thinking?

Man thinks and he imagines that by thinking adequately about the world he can offer a full explanation of it. But he has left out the sheer

marvel that man is able to think so profoundly. Our thought itself,
our capacity to explain everything, is without any explanation.
It belongs to the wonder of existence...

What fills us with radical amazement is not the relations in which everything is embedded but the fact that even the minimum of perception is a maximum of enigma. The most incomprehensible fact is the fact that we comprehend at all.

The way to faith leads through acts of wonder and radical amazement. The words addressed to Job apply to every man:

> Hearken unto this, O Job,
> Stand still and consider the wondrous works of the Lord.
> Do you know how God lays His command upon them,
> And causes the lightning of His cloud to shine?
> Do you know the balancings of the clouds,
> The wondrous works of Him who is perfect in knowledge,
> You whose garments are hot when the earth is still
>   because of the south wind?
> Can you, like Him, spread out the skies,
> Hard as a molten mirror?
> Teach us what we shall say to Him;
> We cannot draw up our case because of darkness.
> Shall it be told Him that I would speak?
> Did a man ever wish that he would be swallowed up?
> And now men cannot look on the light
> When it is bright in the skies
> When the wind has passed and cleared them.
> Out of the north comes golden splendor;
> God is clothed with terrible majesty.
>
> Job 37:14-22

> Come ye and behold the works of God,
> Sublime in His dealing with the sons of men;
>
> Psalms 66:5

The great marvels do not crush the soul; sublimity evokes humility. Looking at the star-studded sky the Psalmist exclaims:

> When I behold Thy heavens, the work of Thy fingers,
> The moon and the stars which Thou hast fashioned—

What is man that Thou shouldst be mindful of him?
And the son of man that Thou shouldst think of him?

Psalms 8:4-5

In radical amazement, the Biblical man faces *"the great things and unsearchable, the wondrous things without number"* **(Job 5:9). He encounters them in space and in time, in nature and in history; not only in the uncommon but also in the common occurrences of nature. Not only do the things outside of him evoke the amazement of the Biblical man; his own being fills him with awe.**

I will give thanks unto Thee
For I am fearfully and marvelously made;
Wondrous are Thy works;
And that my soul knoweth exceedingly.

Psalms 139:14

Heschel quotes the passage from Job in which, without distortion of the text, his thought is implied. The Psalms similarly speak of the sheer wonder of being. This, according to Heschel, is what the Biblical writers have to teach us regarding man's way to God.

The profound and perpetual awareness of the wonder of being has become a part of the religious consciousness of the Jew. Three times a day we pray:

We thank Thee . . .
For Thy miracles which are daily with us,
For Thy continual marvels. . . .

In the evening liturgy we recite the words of Job (9:10):

Who does great things past finding out,
Marvelous things without number.

Every evening we recite: "He creates light and makes the dark." Twice a day we say: "He is One." What is the meaning of such repetition? A scientific theory, once it is announced and accepted, does not have to be repeated twice a day. The insights of wonder must be constantly kept alive. Since there is a need for daily wonder, there is a need for daily worship.

Heschel points out that in the Jewish liturgy, too, the sense of wonder is kept alive. This is why the hymns and praises of God have to be

*repeated so frequently. If it were only a question of knowing a truth,
once or twice would be sufficient. But the whole point of repetition is
to remind ourselves that it is wonderful and there cannot be enough
of this since man tends to take so much for granted. This is an
interesting view of praising God. Does God need our praises? Of
course not, Heschel says, but we need to praise Him and so keep our
sense of wonder alive, which means keeping our souls alive.*

The sense for the "miracles which are daily with us," the sense for
the "continual marvels," is the source of prayer. There is no worship,
no music, no love, if we take for granted the blessings or defeats of
living. No routine of the social, physical, or physiological order must
dull our sense of surprise at the fact that there *is* a social, a physical,
or a physiological order. We are trained in maintaining our sense of
wonder by uttering a prayer before the enjoyment of food. Each time
we are about to drink a glass of water, we remind ourselves of the
eternal mystery of creation, "Blessed be Thou ... by Whose word
all things come into being." A trivial act and a reference to the
supreme miracle. Wishing to eat bread or fruit, to enjoy a pleasant
fragrance or a cup of wine; on tasting fruit in season for the first time;
on seeing a rainbow, or the ocean; on noticing trees when they
blossom; on meeting a sage in Torah or in secular learning; on hearing
good or bad things—we are taught to invoke His great name and our
awareness of Him. Even on performing a physiological function we
say "Blessed be Thou ... who healest all flesh and *doest wonders.*"
*Even a very trivial act like going to sleep and awakening can be a
reminder of how marvellously constructed the human body is and that
is why Jewish tradition demands that we thank God for the
wondrous way our body functions.*

This is one of the goals of the Jewish way of living: to experience
commonplace deeds as spiritual adventures, to feel the hidden love
and wisdom in all things.
  In the Song of the Red Sea we read:

> Who is like Thee, O Lord, among the gods?
> Who is like Thee, majestic in holiness,
> Sublime in glorious deeds, doing wonders.
>
> Exodus 15:11

The Rabbis remarked: It is not written here: *Who did wonders,* **but** *Who does wonders.* . . . **He did and still does wonders for us in every generation, as it is said:**

> **Wondrous are Thy works,**
> **And that my soul knoweth exceedingly.**
> **Psalms 139:14**

Chesterton said that the difference between the poet and the philosopher is that the philosopher tries to get the heavens into his head but the poet tries to get his head into the heavens. For Heschel the whole routine of thanking God for His blessings is to awaken our feelings of poetry and so be led to God. Here there is no argument that believing in God is reasonable. The very fact that one can reason, regardless of where we think it leads us, should already awaken in us a wonder that leads to God.

Relationship is everything

What we mean when we speak to God.

Martin Buber (1878-1965), German Jewish thinker and writer, is one of the most influential forces in twentieth century religious thought. The following selection is from his philosophical poem I and Thou (Authorized English Translation, Ronald Gregor Smith, Charles Scribner's Sons, New York, 1937, Part 3, pages 75-76 and 78-79). A distinguished British philosopher claimed to have read the work through no less than two hundred times!

Men have addressed their eternal *Thou* with many names. In singing of Him who was thus named they always had the *Thou* in mind: the first myths were hymns of praise. Then the names took refuge in the language of *It;* men were more and more strongly moved to think of and to address their eternal *Thou* as an *It*. But all God's names are hallowed, for in them He is not merely spoken about, but also spoken to.

According to Buber there are two kinds of relationship a man can have. When he thinks about something or someone without being personally involved he is said to be thinking of that other person or thing as an It. When he and the other are personally involved, they can be said to be speaking directly to each other. He is then thinking, more precisely he is then relating to, that person or thing as a Thou. Note, not a plural, but a singular; just this other, him and no one in his place. For instance, a man may solemnly sit down to a concert and watch himself enjoying the music. If he can do this he has not really been caught up in the music. He enjoys the music as an It. But if he is so moved that he forgets to think about the music and lets the music speak to him, he then enjoys the music as a Thou. Or to take another example from the sphere of personal relationships. If a man thinks of what use his friend can be to him, even if he loves the friend for this, he is really treating his friend as an It, as an object to be used. But if he finds himself conversing with his friend, exchanging ideas in the spirit of true friendship, when the personality of each speaks to the other, he is treating his friend as a person not a thing. His friend is then for him a Thou. Because they do relate to each other as Thou's, they are truly friends. Thus for Buber every relationship is either an I-Thou relationship or an I-It relationship

Buber would not say that the I-It relationship is unworthy or unimportant. Indeed, in some areas of life it is the only possible way to acquire knowledge. The scientist, for example, must be completely detached when he wishes to study his subject. He thinks about it rather than talks to it. But the only really valid way, says Buber, to get to know persons is through the I-Thou. Buber goes further and claims that surely God is not a thing, to be studied at a distance or used for our purposes. So the only way we can know God is the way we know persons, by the I-Thou. It is ridiculous to imagine that we can get to know much about God by treating Him as an object; but we can speak to Him and He responds. Moreover, according to Buber whenever we attain an I-Thou relationship, with other human beings, for example, God speaks to us too. In every real friendship, in every real love, we are addressing what he calls "the eternal Thou" i.e. the one Thou, God, who can never become an It.

In the above passage Buber says that a name is a form of address. When we say "hello Jack," we are addressing a particular person. So, in a sense, merely by calling him by his name we are speaking to him as a particular individual different from all others. Consequently, whoever uses a name for God, although he might know precious little about God, is addressing Him, nonetheless, as a Thou. It is no accident therefore that the earliest forms of religious address were hymns of praise. In the infancy of the human race men naturally addressed God directly rather than spoke about Him. But later on when men became more sophisticated they began to think more and more about God. This, argues Buber, tends to make God less and less real in human life since He is no longer addressed as Thou.

However, since a name is used, the Thou *is not really lost. It might be argued that early man was not addressing God at all but the gods. Buber would reply that without knowing it these early men were reaching out to the One God and were really bent on addressing Him as the only real Object of worship. He sees truth in very many forms of religion.*

Many men wish to reject the word God as a legitimate usage, because it is so misused. It is indeed the most heavily laden of all the words used by men. For that very reason it is the most imperishable and most indispensable. What does all mistaken talk about God's being and works (though there has been, and can be, no other talk about these) matter in comparison with the one truth that all men who have addressed God had God Himself in mind? For he who speaks the word God and really has *Thou* in mind (whatever the illusion by which he is held), addresses the true *Thou* of his life, which cannot be limited by another *Thou,* and to which he stands in a relation that gathers up and includes all others.

Buber here says that some men wish to give up entirely the use of the word "God" because it means so many different things. For instance, when Hitler said that God was on his side he hardly meant by God what compassionate and just people mean to convey by the word. But Buber says that we ought not to give up this word because it is the word used by men to convey the thought of the Object of their worship and it does not really matter if some men have absurd conceptions (the old man in the sky, for instance). Indeed, all our conceptions cannot really bring us nearer to the reality. But we can approach this reality by addressing God.

The Thou *of God cannot be limited by any other* Thou. *This is not so with regard to human beings. If I have an I-Thou relationship with one person it is somewhat difficult for this not to limit my having a similar relationship with someone else in the same way at the same time. But since God is the "eternal* Thou*" behind all other* Thous*, then His* Thou *is unlimited and whenever I address the "Thou of my life" I am addressing Him.*

But when he, too, who abhors the name, and believes himself to be godless, gives his whole being to addressing the *Thou* of his life, as a *Thou* that cannot be limited by another, he addresses God.

Buber here means that it is possible for a man to address God
without knowing that he does so or without even believing in Him.
Whenever a man really responds to life so that he meets other Thous,
whenever he takes life really seriously and does not merely play
about with it, then, without being aware of it, he has met God. Buber
did not like the word, but what he is saying here is that many
people are more religious than they think.

Every real relation with a being or life in the world is exclusive. Its
***Thou* is freed, steps forth, is single, and confronts you. It fills the**
heavens. This does not mean that nothing else exists; but all else lives
in *its* light. As long as the presence of the relation continues, this its
cosmic range is inviolable. But as soon as a *Thou* becomes *It*, the
cosmic range of the relation appears as an offence to the world, its
exclusiveness as an exclusion of the universe.

In every I-Thou relationship there is the special intimate meeting with
another that makes everything else peripheral to the person
encountered for as long as the relationship lasts. For example, two
people deeply in love with one another are talking together. They may
talk about all sorts of things, which certainly exist for them, but
these exist in the "light" of each other i.e. the whole world becomes,
as it were, part of their I-Thou relationship. This is what Buber means
when he calls the I-Thou "exclusive" and when he says it has a cosmic
range. But when the I-Thou relationship is lost and we are left with
an I-It, then this It becomes one of many, each shutting out the rest.
Buber says this in order to lead up to his next point that God is never
an It, always a Thou, because everything has its being in Him.
Consequently, in man's relationship with God "inclusiveness and
exclusiveness are one."

In the relation with God unconditional exclusiveness and uncondi-
tional inclusiveness are one. He who enters on the absolute relation
is concerned with nothing isolated any more, neither things nor
beings, neither earth nor heaven; but everything is gathered up in the
relation. For to step into pure relation is not to disregard everything
but to see everything in the *Thou*, not to renounce the world but to
establish it on its true basis. To look away from the world, or to stare
at it, does not help a man to reach God; but he who sees the world

in Him stands in His presence. "Here world, there God" is the language of _It;_ "God in the world" is another language of _It;_ but to eliminate or leave behind nothing at all, to include the whole world in the _Thou,_ to give the world its due and its truth, to include nothing beside God but everything in Him—this is full and complete relation.

The "absolute relation" is man's relationship with God. Buber disagrees with the mystical approach, for example, in which man comes to know God by going beyond the world. Since God embraces everything there is in the world, to approach God as Thou is to approach all the world which is included in His Thou. When a man says: "Here is God, there is the world" he treats God as a being among others. In Buber's language he sees God as an It. And this applies, too, to the man who speaks of "God in the world." He, too, sees God and the world as two separate entities. But in the I-Thou relationship. man sees the whole world through that relationship with God and there is no longer any exclusion of the world. Remember the illustration given earlier of the lover who sees the whole world through the eyes of his beloved. The great problem of religion is to see God while remaining in the world. Anyone who simply embraces life in the world without thinking of God at all obviously misses the religious point. But by the same token anyone who tries to see God by escaping from the world sets up an artificial division, as it were, between God and the world. It prevents him from seeing God through the world but that is the only place in which He can be seen. The solution for Buber is neither to see the world without God nor God without the world but to see the world as embraced by God's Thou. All this is extremely difficult because it is so personal and many thinkers would refuse to put it quite in Buber's way.

Men do not find God if they stay in the world. They do not find Him if they leave the world. He who goes out with his whole being to meet his _Thou_ and carries to it all being that is in the world, finds Him who cannot be sought.

Buber means that since God's nature is utterly incomprehensible it is a waste of time trying to find Him as He is in Himself i.e. by trying to discover Him apart from the world. The religious man finds God in the real world of everybody. God can only be known as He "speaks" to man through worldly things. Hence by reaching out to Him as a Thou man brings all the world to Him.

Of course God is the "wholly Other"; but He is also the wholly Same, the wholly Present. Of course He is the *Mysterium Tremendum* that appears and overthrows; but He is also the mystery of the self-evident, nearer to me than my *I*.

Buber has said that God is to be approached through the world, by meeting His Thou in the world. But, now he asks, is God not completely beyond the world? Yes, he replies, this is certainly so, but He is also in the world He has created. The terms "wholly Other" and Mysterium Tremendum (tremendous mystery) are used by religious thinkers when speaking of God as apart from the world. From this point of view, God is utterly different from anything we can know and is so mysterious that we cannot hope to know Him as He really is. When He appears He "overthrows" i.e. He overpowers us by His presence because it is so tremendously different from anything in our experience. Buber accepts all this but adds that there is another mystery and that is God's nearness, i.e. that He is to be found everywhere in the world. Buber's phrase "nearer to me than my I" is quite provocative.

If you explore the life of things and of conditioned being you come to the unfathomable, if you deny the life of things and of conditioned being you stand before nothingness, if you hallow this life you meet the living God.

Buber sums up his point of view. "Conditioned being" is the being of all things we see. All that we know has a "condition" i.e. it depends on something else. This book, for instance, is here because the publishers produce it. The publishers are its "condition." But they, too, are "conditioned" i.e. a reason has to be found why they are here, in this case, one answer would be because of their parents. In this way we can go on and on asking for the "conditions" and eventually we come to a point where we can give no more answers, where there are only questions. Sooner or later, strictly speaking, the reason for things is unfathomable. Similarly, if one tries to deny that there are any "things," this is an attempt to deny the world of experience (there have been thinkers who have tried to teach that somehow the whole world is a colossal illusion) and it leads to nothingness. Both ways, searching things or denying them, will get us nowhere. The answer, as Buber has repeatedly stated, is to hallow the world of things i.e. to approach it in the open way one goes to meet a friend. When one does this one meets with the "living God," that is the

God who is the Thou one meets in the life of the world. Buber thus affirms the value of life in this world and does not follow those religious thinkers who feel that God is only to be found if one gets away from worldly things. Buber in his personal life always expressed this idea. He liked to dress well, for instance, and was rather fond of showy ties. But he did not care about your dress or position but who you really were. He believed that everything we experience is part of God's creation and therefore if approached as a Thou can bring us into a dialogue (a word of which Buber was particularly fond) with God. This is not what we normally consider the approach of reason, but it is not unreasonable. This is not the way of wonder or any sort of experience not tied to the other. It is Buber's quite unique way of thinking and living.

Our God affects our life

The significance of God for a modern man.

Mordecai Kaplan was born in Lithuania in 1881 and was brought to the United States at the age of eight. He became one of the most influential Rabbis and educators in the Western World and the founder of the Reconstructionist movement. Kaplan's thought is based on the need to interpret Jewish values in accordance with the ideas of the modern age, particularly stressing the new outlook on human life afforded us in a scientific age. The following selection is from Kaplan's regular feature in the magazine The Reconstructionist *in which, like any good teacher, he conveyed his philosophy in reply to questions submitted to him. These were published in a book titled* Questions Jews Ask *(New York, 1956, pp. 82-5).*

Whatever general idea we hold in our minds and regard as pointing to, or representative, of Reality, or of any phase of it, derives from something seen, heard, felt, believed or assumed. . . . That fact is true also of the belief in God. In most religions of the past, that belief was derived from *traditions* concerning self-revelations of God through visions and oracles. Those traditions are now discounted by all who have become habituated to scientific and philosophic thought. Though such people are in the minority, their influence is bound to increase with time, and their rejection of the traditional basis of the belief in God is certain to be followed by a like attitude on the part of the multitude. This may take a long time, but it is bound to come sooner or later.

Kaplan first states the problem as he sees it. He starts by pointing out that all our knowledge proceeds from something we know to something we do not know. We infer the unknown from the known. Thus belief in God—the unknown—must proceed from that which we know to be so. In the past men believed that this known aspect was a vision of God, as described in the Bible, for instance. But according to Kaplan, many thinkers nowadays would reject this as a basis of knowledge because, to be frank, there is no real evidence that any such vision ever took place. Men in a scientific age demand proof and this is not forthcoming. All we have are stories of God revealing Himself to man. A modern, scientific man will treat these stories with skepticism because they belong to an age in which strong evidence was not required before accepting marvelous tales as true. Here we find Kaplan supremely confident of the methods of science and his whole way of thinking is based on this. Others have challenged his brave dismissal of the miraculous.

Those who are not content with the superficiality of merely rejecting a belief that has been so universal, spontaneous and persistent as the belief in God, have turned their attention to the study of human nature and its needs. They have rightly concluded that there must be something in the very nature of man which has led him to create that vast and complex edifice of religion with its creeds, rituals, institutions and politics. What is that something? Some maintain that religion is the product of fear of whatever is beyond man's control, and that it is nothing but a disguised form of primitive magic to which man resorted, expecting the supposed gods, demons, spirits and angels to fulfill his wishes. As man learns to bring under control more and more of the forces in his own body and in his environment, he feels he can dispense with religion, or belief in God; what he cannot control, he has to accept with resignation. Others, however, and I among them, assume that man, once his physiological needs are satisfied, begins to experience the need to overcome such traits as self-indulgence, arrogance, envy, exploitation and hatred, or to bring under control the aggressive forces of his nature. That constitutes man's true destiny. Therein lies his salvation.

Since, as Kaplan has argued, the evidence of God accepted by the ancients can no longer be accepted, the question to be considered is why in that case has religion persisted for so long. Why have so many millions of people believed in God and practiced religious ceremonies if there is nothing in reality to correspond with God? One answer given, for example, by Freud, is that, indeed, religion is an illusion and was originally based on fear. Primitive man was so bothered by his fear of death, of accidents, of earthquakes and other disasters, and so little able to control these, that he forced himself into believing that he could control the world by practising magic. On this view religion is only a kind of magic and should be abandoned now that man has learned to a large extent to exercise control over his world. Instead of praying to God for good health, he encourages doctors to advance the cause of medicine. But Kaplan finds himself unable to accept this. Man has two kinds of needs. First there are his physical needs. These he can to a large extent control. But man has not learned how to control his aggressive instincts. He wishes to harm others and yet recognizes that life should be lived on a higher plane than this. Religion is still as vital as ever it was in encouraging man to rise above his natural instincts and lead a better life. This is why religion persists—because it caters to one of man's deepest needs. Kaplan goes on to say that this is, in fact, the true force behind religion and when men said that they believed in God what they were really saying, perhaps without knowing it, was that the universe is so constituted that man is able to live worthily and nobly if he wants to. A thinker who argued much as Kaplan does in this matter was Ludwig Feuerbach in the last century. Feuerbach once said that when men said "God is good" what they were really saying was "Good is God."

From that point, it is natural to arrive at the next step, which requires no blind leap into the dark. The next step is to conclude that the cosmos is so constituted as to enable man to fulfill this highest human need of his nature.

Kaplan is suspicious of any religious faith based on the idea of a leap into the dark i.e. on that for which there is no evidence whatsoever. He does not believe that his kind of faith is such an unwarranted leap because it is plausible to argue that if man has these higher needs to live nobly then there must be something in the universe which can help him so to live. This power or force in the universe Kaplan calls God: not a "person," a "being," but real nonetheless.

A magnetic needle, hung on a thread or placed on a pivot, assumes of its own accord a position in which one end of the needle points north

and the other south. So long as it is free to move about, all attempts to deflect it will not get it to remain away from its normal direction. Likewise, man normally veers in the direction of that which makes for the fulfillment of his destiny as a human being. That fact indicates the functioning of a cosmic Power which influences his behavior. What magnetism is to the magnetic needle, Godhood or God is to man.

No one will deny that there is a magnetic force in the universe which moves the needle, even though we do not understand adequately the exact nature of that force. Similarly, since man appears to be so constituted that he is always striving for a nobler life, we are justified in concluding that the universe itself is so constituted that it contains the force which moves him in this direction. Man's striving for that which makes him noble and truly human, for his true fulfillment, Kaplan calls his "salvation." Hence his famous definition of God as "The Power that makes for salvation." Kaplan obviously has a very high estimate of human nature.

To carry the analogy one step further, just as the magnetic needle is the source of our knowledge of the earth's magnetism, so is man's salvational behavior the source of our knowledge of God. And just as we learn from the action of the magnetic needle the laws of magnetism so do we learn from man's salvational behavior, which we come progressively really to understand, the law or will of God.

For Kaplan God's will is not something revealed to man from without, but we call God's will that which we notice from man's nature and conduct which enables him to find his highest fulfillment, his "salvation." For instance, the traditional view is that God revealed to man the law stating "Thou shalt not steal." Kaplan would understand this rather that, since men who do steal are wretched, not alone do they harm others but they find no peace in themselves, it is clear that they are not in tune with the universe as it is constituted. It can therefore be concluded that the Power which makes for salvation is opposed to stealing, or, better, that stealing is out of tune with that Power. We call this God's law or His will that man should not steal.

There is, to be sure, a large element of faith in the foregoing type of analogical reasoning. But it is the kind of faith without which we could not live. When we count upon the sun's rising tomorrow morning, we act upon that kind of indispensable faith. You cannot compare that kind of faith to faith in the Biblical story that the sun stood still for Joshua. Likewise, you cannot say that faith in God as the process that makes man's salvation possible, is as "unprovable" as faith in an anthropomorphic God. For that matter, the human person, too, is not a ghost double of each of us, that walks out on us when we go to bed. The human person, too, is part of the salvation-making process, and is as much an object of faith as is God.

By an "anthropomorphic God" Kaplan means a God who is thought of simply as a gigantic man. He prefers to think of God as a Power or a Process. He quotes the illustration of the human being himself. We may say that someone has a soul, he is so good and kindly. This surely does not mean that inside his body there is a kind of midget which resembles his body. In fact, we cannot describe the nature of the soul. Yet we have faith that there is such a thing since this is the way we understand kindliness and goodness. It is all part of the salvation-making process which we accept on faith but on a faith that is founded in our experience.

The universality and persistence of religion, in whatever form it has manifested itself, can thus be easily accounted for. Even the intellectuals who claim that religion has been motivated by fear and by the attempt to bring under control the inexplorable elements in the world, experience this highest need of human nature, the need for salvation, however they conceive it. Though they do not articulate it through worship, they seek some outlet like poetry, art or a social cause. All this implies that human life, and the cosmos, which is its source, demand more of man than that he be able to split the atom or traverse the interplanetary spaces.

Kaplan means here that man is clearly not entirely satisfied with the power to control the outside world, but he has a real need to find the highest within himself, what Kaplan has called "salvation."

The fact that the cosmos possesses the resources and man the abilities —which are themselves part of those resources—to enable him to fulfill his destiny as a human being, or to achieve salvation—is the Godhood of the cosmos. That is the fact we should have in mind when we worship God and glorify Him in inexhaustible variations on the motif of "Halleluyah." Even when we conceive God as Process, we do not pray to a *what* or to a *fact*. **When we pray, we** *affirm the* **what or** *the* **fact that spells salvation. Likewise, when we address ourselves to God in prayer of petition, we raise to the level of consciousness those desires, the fulfillment of which we regard as a prerequisite to the fulfillment of our human destiny.**

Critics of Kaplan have asked how prayer is possible to a Process. We can praise a Person or ask Him to grant our needs, but is it not comical to pray to a thing? Kaplan answers that we do not, in fact, pray to the Process but we call our own attention to it so that we might always strive for the highest.

All the theologians who deprecate the naive conception of God as an anthropomorphic being, virtually do not themselves believe in God as an identifiable being or entity. When they denounce the notion of God as Process, they apparently try to convey the impression that their own idea of God is at least comprehensible. Actually, they keep on stressing at the same time that God is absolutely unknowable, in-scrutable, and ineffable. They use the very terms in which the agnostic Herbert Spencer long ago described God. They keep on repeating that we can know God only through His manifestations, or that He reveals Himself not in objects, but in events. What are manifestations and events, if not process? These theologians are merely hurling at the notion of God as Process the same anathemas that have been hurled at the God idea of the medieval theologians by the naive pietists who conceived of God in human form.

Some people have the very naive concept of God as an "old man in the sky" and so forth. The great medieval thinkers such as Maimonides urged men to depart from this ridiculous idea and purify the idea of God for which they were attacked by the naive pietists. Kaplan believes that his attempt to describe God in terms of Process is a further purification of the God idea and the one most acceptable to modern man.

Beyond anthropomorphism

What it means to say that God is a Person.

Rabbi Isidore Epstein (1894-1960) was the Principal of Jews' College, London, editor of the Soncino translation of the whole of the Babylonian Talmud into English, the author of a number of books advocating the Orthodox Jewish viewpoint. The following selection is taken from his book: The Faith of Judaism *(London, 1954, pages 136-139; 143-145).*

The whole Jewish religion revolves around the acceptance of the existence of a "personal" God. By this is meant the affirmation that what controls our life is not a blind force of which we know little, or nothing, but a supreme Being which, although beyond our imagining, is yet possessed of intelligence, purpose, will and other excellent qualities which we are wont to associate with the term "personality." Of course, we may say—nay, we must say—that the term "personality" is totally inadequate to describe God. It is a term too much limited by its human associations to be applied to God. We nevertheless use it of God, because the word "personality" expresses the "most glorious" form of existence with which we are acquainted; and when we speak of God as a person, we mean that God is not an impersonal force. He is not a mere force or law, not an It, but a He.

This must be insisted upon, as we could not, as persons, have any relationship, such as that which constitutes the essence of all religious belief, with an impersonal force.. An impersonal God must remain impervious to human prayers and supplications, and cannot be possessed of any of those higher values we strive to realise in our lives. It was in order to awaken and to safeguard this sense of personal relation with God that the Bible did not hesitate to resort to anthropomorphic descriptions of God, ascribing to Him attributes of a Person. The very word "personality," however, explain it as you will, is suggestive of limitations and imperfections. To obviate these religiously dangerous implications, Judaism emphasises the incorporeality of God, as all limitations and imperfections in human personality are imposed in a large measure by the body that envelops it; and forbids the making of any image of God. God is thus affirmed to be Pure Spirit. It is, of course, impossible for us to envisage a spirit, as our experience does not reach out to something which cannot be seen, touched or felt; but neither can the human spirit, the soul, the life that fills the human body, as well as everything around us, be seen.

It will be seen at once that Epstein is totally opposed to Kaplan's views recorded above. Although Kaplan is not mentioned in this section of the work, Epstein earlier (on page 77) refers to Kaplan's philosophy as "the entire elimination of the supernatural from religion" and dubs it "a travesty of the Jewish religion." Note how both Kaplan and Epstein give the illustration of the human soul, each using the illustration for his own purpose. Epstein wishes to affirm the idea of personality but he is also aware that this, or, indeed, any such terms, are inapplicable to God. Epstein now brings a quotation from the Chandogya Upanishad, quoted in A. Huxley: Perennial Philosophy (1947), page 9. This is a Hindu work, but Epstein believes that in this matter the Chandogya Upanishad is giving expression to a view that would be accepted by Judaism.

' "Bring me a fruit from that tree'. "Here it is, venerable Sir." "Cut it open." "It is cut open, venerable Sir." "What seest thou in it?" "Very small seeds, venerable Sir." "Cut open one of them." "It is cut open, venerable Sir." "What seest thou in it?" "Nothing, venerable Sir." Then spake he, "That hidden thing which thou seest not, O gentle youth, from that hidden thing verily has this mighty tree grown." '

Indeed, He whom we see not is the source and life of all being. In fact the human soul provides the Sages of the Talmud with the nearest analogy after which God is best conceived.

"As the soul fills the body, so God fills the world; as the soul sustains the body, so God sustains the world; as the soul sees but is not seen, so God sees but is not seen."

It will be noted that the analogy between God and the soul, as applied by the Talmudic Sages, goes beyond the mere idea of God as the invisible source of existence. It also serves to illustrate the conception of the immanence of God, that is, His omnipresence, which has ever been recognised as fundamental to Jewish doctrine: "As the soul fills the human body, so God fills the world." The immanence of God is a dominant tenet of Jewish religious faith. Already in the Bible we find this truth affirmed over and over again in no uncertain terms. "Can any man hide himself in secret places that I should not see him? saith the Lord, Do I not fill Heaven and earth?" (Jeremiah 23:24). "The fullness of the whole earth is His glory" (Isaiah 6:3).—His glory (Kabod) denoting here the manifestation of the Divine presence. Or, as the Psalmist so beautifully expresses it,

> Whither shall I go from Thy spirit?
> Or whither shall I flee from Thy presence?
> If I ascend up to Heaven, Thou art there,
> If I make my bed in the nether-world, behold,
>   Thou art there.
> If I take the wings of the morning,
> And dwell in the uttermost parts of the sea,
> Even there would Thy hand lead me,
> And Thy right hand would hold me

> (Psalms 139:7-10)

The teaching of the Bible is equally the doctrine of Rabbinic Judaism. So deeply conscious were the Rabbis of the all-pervading presence of God, that they coined a special term to describe it. This term is Shechinah, which means literally, "Indwelling." "The Shechinah is everywhere," "there is no place devoid of the Shechinah"—are some of the dicta by which they sought to give expression to this overwhelming sense which they had of God's omnipresence. The thought of divine immanence also suffuses the whole of the Jewish mystic literature. Among the most impressive utterances in this connection may be quoted the one in the "Song of Unity."

> "Everything is in Thee, and Thou art everything.
> Thou fillest everything and dost encompass it.

When everything was created, Thou wast everything,
Before everything was created, Thou wast everything."

In his notes to this this passage Epstein remarks that an "extremely
valuable contribution to the idea of Divine Immanence in Rabbinic
teaching is J. Abelson, Immanence of God in Rabbinical Literature
(1912)" and that the Unity Hymn "was composed by members of the
inner circle round R. Judah he-Hasid (d. 1217)." We now skip a few
paragraphs (in which Epstein describes how God is transcendent
as well as immanent i.e. He is beyond the world as well as within it)
and go on to the section where he takes up again the theme of
the Divine "personality."

Much is heard to-day of the age-old reluctance to attribute personality to God. Modern writers prefer to speak of God as impersonal;
the assumption being that by this usage a higher plane of thought is
reached than that common to the highest religions, which are stigma-
tized as anthropomorphic in that they make God in the image of man.
A typical representative of this attitude is Julian Huxley, who in his
book, *Religion without Revelation,* pleads for the "liberation of the
idea of God from the shackles of personality," and expresses his conviction that "religion of the highest and fullest character can co-exist
with a complete absence of belief in revelation in any straight-forward
sense of the word, and in that kernel of revealed religion, namely a
personal God."

This problem is nowadays much discussed e.g. in the best-selling
paperback by the Bishop of Woolwich, John Robinson, titled:
Honest to God.

What exactly he means by God, after denying to Him His attributes of
personality, Huxley does not attempt to explain. The best he can say
on the subject is that "God is one name for the Universe as it impinges
on our lives." Neither does he adduce any reason for retaining belief
in a God who is non-personal, and with whom one cannot enter into
personal relationship. Huxley is apparently not unaware of the difficulty, and he seeks to fill the void thus created by affirming the
existence of a spiritual Universe, possessed of spiritual values, such as
truth, beauty, goodness, which should call forth our love and reverence. He does not, however, seem to realise that to speak of a spiritual
Universe that is non-personal, involves a contradiction in terms. Spiri-

tual values are, after all, centered in personality, and it is meaningless to talk of spiritual values without the association of a living personality. Intelligence, ethical concepts or values are perceptible only in personalities, and can emanate from, and be expressed only by, personalities. And so is an impersonal deity a contradiction in terms. It may be a materialistic deity, but not one of "high religious maturity." Once he is deprived of will, purpose, and other such attributes that constitute personality, he becomes like the idols of the heathens of old that have ears and hear not, eyes and see not. Nor will any amount of refinement or sublimation of his essence endow him with a spiritual quality. He will remain a material being, mechanical in his behaviour and with reactions not different to that of electricity or gravitation.

Above, in the selection from Kaplan's writings, he tries to grapple with the kind of criticism put forward here by Epstein.

It will have become evident that religion has no meaning without the postulate of a "personal" God. Nor has a spiritual Universe any significance without the recognition of a personality behind the scheme of things. The mistake of these moderns who recoil from the thought of ascribing personality to God, is to confuse "personality" and "corporeality." In fact the two are quite separate and distinct. "Corporeality" is restrictive; "personality" is expansive. "Corporeality" is quantitative; "personality" is qualitative. "Corporeality" is instrumental; "personality" is functional. What imparts to a mind personality is not the hands, the eyes, the brain, but the power to organise, direct and unify the various component parts of the body into one single purpose and goal. Personality is mind become autonomous—mind become emancipated from bondage to the body. If the Universe has a mind, that mind would be more, rather than less, personal than our own. For it would have more, rather than less, unity and organicity.

It should perhaps be said here that there is no word in classical Hebrew for "personality" but Epstein is certainly right that in the classical sources the idea of a Divine Person is always presented. The trouble is that if this is taken too literally anthropomorphism (the description of God in human terms) results. The question then is how far should one go in negating the personal aspect and how far in affirming it. This is really at the heart of the difference between Kaplan and Epstein, with Epstein's view indubitably the more traditional. One might also say that the difference between them centers on how much importance should be given to science. Kaplan thinks science ought to give us a basic way of thinking about man and religion. Epstein feels science fails us just when it comes to man. It would reduce personality to heredity and learning, not leaving much room for man's freedom or the uniqueness of his kind of being. So Epstein refuses to reduce men to mere complicated organisms. Rather he sees human beings in their special complexity as getting us closer to God and ultimate reality. Thus rather than speak of God in terms of physical science, Epstein, with some safeguards, says that we will do best by speaking of Him on the basis of what it means to be a person.

CHAPTER 6

BAECK: THE ESSENCE OF JUDAISM

Love is more than thinking

*The difference between saying that God exists
and really believing in God.*

*Leo Baeck (1873-1959) was a great German Jewish leader and thinker.
He wrote* The Essence of Judaism *(a rendition by Irving Howe based
on the translation of Victor Grubenwieser and Leonard Pearl,
Schocken Books Inc., 1948) as his detailed statement of what Judaism
means. The following on the Jewish doctrine of God (pages 97-100)
examines the way Judaism understands this idea but gives no
references to the sources. Nevertheless Baeck could rightly claim that
his ideas are all based on teachings found in the classical Jewish
sources.*

Certain thinkers have paradoxically maintained that the idea of God
is in itself no more religious than, say, the idea of gravitation. There
is a certain truth in this view. For it is possible to accept the existence
of a God on philosophical grounds to explain the cosmic order by
establishing a first cause in the process of nature. Toward that concept
of God, the paradox is justified. The philosophical formula of God as
the first mover is in itself not really richer in religious significance than
any other philosophical idea. In this idea faith can find neither its
basis nor strength. The gift of religious certainty is conveyed solely by
that which God means to our existence and our soul, by the inner consistency which our life thus gains, by our resultant moral power, by

34

the satisfaction of finding answers to our questions and demands, and by our discovery of the relationship between our spiritual nature and the Divine—that feeling which realizes the call from God to us each day of our lives: "Where art thou?" (Gen. 3:9).

A number of arguments or proofs have been brought from time to time in the history of philosophy to demonstrate that there is a God. Thus one argument runs that there must be a God otherwise how did the universe come into being. Baeck insists that mere acceptance of this kind of argument does not make a man religious. Such a man accepts that there is a God just as he accepts any other proposition which his reason tells him is true, the theory of gravitation, for example. If we look at the life of a truly religious person we see much more to his life than a bare assertion that there is a God. He tries to live in accordance with God's laws, that is to say, he tries to be honest, kind and just because he believes that this is what God wants him to do. He prays to God and so has a relationship with Him. God meets him, as it were, at every turn, urging him to strive always to be better. There is far more warmth and commitment in true belief than a bare acceptance of the proposition "God exists." We know, for example, that our neighbor exists, but we are not a good neighbor to him until he enters our lives and we his, until we have a relationship with him. "Where art thou?" is the question put by God to Adam (Genesis 3:9). This whole way of approach is called nowadays the "existentialist" i.e. what matters is not the fact itself but how it has its effect on our "existence," on how we live with the truth.

For Judaism, religion does not consist simply in the recognition of God's existence. We possess religion only when we know that our life is bound up with something eternal, when we feel that we are linked with God and that he is our God. And he is our God, as the phrase has it, if we love him, if we find through him our trust and humility, our courage and our peace, if we lay ourselves open in our innermost being to his revelation and commandment. Our attempts to grasp and express this inner connection are always only in the form of a simile— an expression of the human soul. Our praise of God, with its use of "I" and "Thou," shapes the features of ourselves, and our meditations about God, with its use of the word "He," forms our idea of him. But whether we approach God with devout words of intimacy or we desire to approach God by pure thought, the result is essentially the same so long as we feel that he is our God. Of our God our minds may form their own conceptions and ideas and our hearts may concurrently pray to him: "Thou, O Lord, art our Father, our Redeemer; thy name is from everlasting" (Isa. 63:16). "Whom have I in heaven but Thee? And there is none upon earth that I desire beside Thee. My flesh and my heart faileth: but God is the strength of my heart, and my portion for ever" (Ps. 73:25f.). That is why Judaism speaks so little of religious doctrine and confessions of faith, but speaks rather of the living God, who is God to every man. Only thus does the idea of God become a religious one, only thus does it gain its religious strength. To know of this One God, in whom all things find meaning, to bear witness to him, to trust in him, to find shelter in him, to believe in him—that is what Israel taught mankind and that constitutes the monotheism which its prophets gave to the world.

Judaism does not speak much of arguments for the existence of God because God was so real to the great Hebrew prophets that it would have seemed absurd to them to prove that He existed. In any event, as Baeck has said, the heart of true religion is not in the bare affirmation that there is a God but in the relationship man has to Him. This is what Baeck means by our God. He is not simply God, without any relevance to our lives, but our God. We can approach Him either by means of prayer in which we use intimate terms like "Thou" or we can think about Him, approach Him in thought. But whichever way we do approach Him, if there is real concern in the way we do it we can be said to be engaging in religious activity. By "simile" Baeck means that a human being can never really know the nature of God so that he is bound to think of his relationship with God as we would of any other relationship. He is using symbolic or figurative language. Whatever he says of God is "simile."

The characteristic feature of Judaism is thus the relation of man to God. Essential to it is the consciousness of being created. This conception is uniquely Jewish, peculiar to the belief in the One God. When man faces fate and nature and their gods, he feels himself dependent upon them in both the accidents and occurrences of his life; he is compelled and driven by neutral forces, wholly elect or wholly rejected. But when he faced the One God, the Israelite felt quite differently: for he knew himself to have been created by God, created just as everything else had been created. His life, and the lives of all others, thus became for him the revelation of the One God; in the religious sense, revelation and creation are the same. Israel was filled with the consciousness of being united with the One who is different from everything else, of being embraced and sustained by him, of knowing that in him lies the answer to the secret of man's origin and of all that exists. And thereby man experiences in himself the meaning of the entire world. Man and the world are linked in one certainty of life, a conviction that all life was bestowed, is upheld and will be maintained in safety forever. The One God is the God of the beginning and the end; he is *my* God. "The earth is the Lord's and the fullness thereof, the world and they that dwell therein" (Ps. 24:1). In place of the mythological legends of formation and annihilation there is here the idea of creation, the spiritual experience of the relation of all things human, all the world and all time with the one living God. In place of fatalism, which shows only the abysses of the inevitable, there is the idea of God in his creation. The mystery of growth becomes the certainty of origin and life. Not contingent events, but creation and divine action characterize the principle of the world.

Man cannot possibly have any consciousness of God's nature. What he can have is a consciousness that he has been created by God together with everything else there is. Baeck considers the Jewish teaching regarding creation as of the utmost significance. In the pagan mythologies there was no doctrine of creation. There was only "formation and annihilation" i.e., gods were formed, worlds were formed, and then these gave way to other gods and other worlds and the whole obeyed inevitable laws. Given such a picture man could only bow to his fate. He might be "saved" i.e. it might have been fated that he would be happy or it might be fated otherwise. In any event he could himself do nothing about it, any more than the gods could do. But when Judaism teaches that everything has been created by the One God all is quite different. The world is not fated to work out a pattern determined for it from the beginning or rather there is scope within God's patterns for man's own efforts. He is free and his life has meaning. The sense the Israelite had of being created by God was his sense of God revealing Himself to him. Just as God created the whole world out of nothing He still controls the whole world so that when man is close to God he is at one and the same time nearer to understanding the meaning of life and free from utter dependence on the world and its accidents. For such a man things do not merely happen. God causes them to happen. Baeck's phrase *"abysses of the inevitable" means that in a fatalistic picture there are abysses into which man cannot help falling. It is all inevitable.*

With this consciousness of being created there enters into man's finite and transient life the feeling of infinitude and eternity. The nature of the creating God is beyond all human knowledge and conjecture—therein lies the feeling of his infinitude and eternity—but our life derives from him, so that we are related and near to him. Though we are as "dust and ashes" (Gen. 18:27) when compared to God, we nevertheless belong to him; though he is unfathomable and inscrutable, yet we emanate from him. The feeling of the dark secret becomes the feeling of infinite protection. That which lies hidden and that in which we are securely sheltered—the eternal secret and the eternal protection—are one word in biblical language. All existence is seen in relation to the unconditioned, the infinite and eternal; created life receives its significance from God. Though it is the realm of the mortal, the world is nevertheless the world of God; he is the Holy One and yet God of the world. "Holy, holy, holy, is the Lord of Hosts, the whole earth is full of his glory" (Isa. 6:3). This becomes the experience of the man who realizes that the One God is his God and who therefore grasps the meaning of all life in his own life. The connection between the manifold and the One, the transitory and the eternal, the apparent and the unfathomable is now established. Between God and man and between God and the world, a covenant is established; the world, like man, is given its place in religion.

Man has a consciousness of having been created, as Baeck has said. The result of this is that he knows he has been brought into being by God. But God is not bound by the world or by time, both of which He created. Therefore, man, too, since he knows that he has been created by God, has some feeling of connection with infinity and eternity i.e. with that which is beyond all time and the whole universe. Although man in relation to God is only "dust and ashes" (see Genesis 18:27) yet he is "dust and ashes" created by God and therefore is close, as it were, to God's eternity. The "dark secret" i.e., the utter mystery of God's nature becomes a source of protection for man. Man can never feel hopelessly lost in the world because his life is linked with the God who is more than and beyond the world. Baeck's remarks about the "one word" probably refer to the fact that in Hebrew the same word olam is used both for "world" and "eternity."

The root of this word can mean "to be hidden." Hence Baeck says that the world we see all around us was brought into being by the "hidden" God and this gives to the world, too, as it were, something of God's eternity.

The idea of a covenant, found so frequently in the Bible, is a metaphor when used of God and man or God and the world. God does not actually write out a deed of covenant, a contract, as a man does—but expresses the deepest truth that there is a relationship between God and man and God and the world. This idea can be extended also to the idea of creation. By creating the world God makes a kind of "covenant" with it. The world is linked to God's eternity since it has been created by Him and it thus is given a place in religion. It cannot be pretended that Baeck's thought is easy and it is perhaps a pity that he was not able to express his meaning more clearly but what is clear is Baeck's sense that believing in God must be a very personal and intimate thing. Baeck insists that if we realize that our time is short, that we are transients in the world, brought into it not by ourselves and supported in it not by ourselves but by God, then we will have the sort of minute by minute living of our lives with God that Judaism desires.

The old God and the new evils

How the problem of evil makes us revise
our idea of God.

The magazine Commentary, *in the August 1966 issue, published a*
symposium on Jewish beliefs. One of the questions asked was:
Does the so-called "God is dead" question which has been agitating
Christian theologians have any relevance to Judaism? *The following*
reply is by Richard L. Rubenstein. In this and in other writings
Rubenstein explores the idea that, indeed, it is very hard today,
particularly in view of the Holocaust, to believe in the traditional
conception of God.

No man can really say that God is dead. How can we know that?
Nevertheless, I am compelled to say that we live in the time of the
"death of God." This is more a statement about man and his culture
than about God. The death of God is a cultural fact. Buber felt this.
He spoke of the eclipse of God. I can understand his reluctance to use
the more explicitly Christian terminology. I am compelled to utilize it
because of my conviction that the time which Nietzsche's madman
said was too far off has come upon us. There is no way around
Nietzsche. Had I lived in another time or another culture, I might have
found some other vocabulary to express my meanings. I am, however,
a religious existentialist after Nietzsche and after Auschwitz. When I
say we live in the time of the death of God, I mean that the thread

uniting God and man, heaven and earth, has been broken. We stand in a cold, silent, unfeeling cosmos, unaided by any purposeful power beyond our own resources. After Auschwitz, what else can a Jew say about God?

Rubenstein believes that after Auschwitz, the terrible extermination camp, and the other horrors of the Nazi period, when six million innocent Jews were slaughtered, it is impossible for a Jew to affirm that there is a God who is benevolent and cares for His creatures. This is the burning problem of evil with which believers in God have always had to grapple, but for Rubenstein the sheer magnitude of the problem nowadays demands a far more radical approach than anything advanced so far. The German philosopher Nietzsche, at the end of the last century, said that a time would come when men would know that "God is dead." He imagines a madman going around with a torch looking for God and telling men that He is no longer to be found. Rubenstein prefers to speak of the death of God rather than say, as Buber did, that God has been eclipsed—because the latter suggests that He is, after all, quite real and, once the moments of eclipse are past, He will be seen again.

I believe the greatest single challenge to modern Judaism arises out of the question of God and the death camps. I am amazed at the silence of contemporary Jewish theologians on this most crucial and agonizing of all Jewish issues. How can Jews believe in an omnipotent, beneficent God after Auschwitz? Traditional Jewish theology maintains that God is the ultimate, omnipotent actor in the historical drama. It has interpreted every major catastrophe in Jewish history as God's punishment of a sinful Israel. I fail to see how this position can be maintained without regarding Hitler and the SS as instruments of God's will. The agony of European Jewry cannot be likened to the testing of Job. To see any purpose in the death camps, the traditional believer is forced to regard the most demonic, antihuman explosion in all history as a meaningful expression of God's purposes. The idea is simply too obscene for me to accept. I do not think that the full impact of Auschwitz has yet been felt in Jewish theology or Jewish life. Great religious revolutions have their own period of gestation. No man knows the hour when the full impact of Auschwitz will be felt, but no religious community can endure so hideous a wounding without undergoing vast inner disorders.

Rubenstein means here that when a single individual, like Job in the Bible, suffers undeservedly it is possible to make some sense out of the suffering e.g., it might show how a good man keeps his faith even in the face of terrible suffering. In other words it could have been maintained that even a wholly good God has some purpose when He permits humans to suffer. But in the case of the holocaust this would mean for Rubenstein that God has used the SS and the rest as instruments for the fulfillment of His purpose and he finds this an "obscene" idea to be totally rejected.

Though I believe that a void stands where once we experienced God's presence, I do not think Judaism has lost its meaning or its power. I do not believe that a theistic God is necessary for Jewish religious life. Dietrich Bonhoeffer has written that our problem is how to speak of God in an age of no religion. I believe that our problem is how to speak of religion in an age of no God. I have suggested that Judaism is the way in which we share the decisive times and crises of life through the traditions of our inherited community. The need for that sharing is not diminished in the time of the death of God. We no longer believe in the God who has the power to annul the tragic necessities of existence; the need religiously to share that existence remains.

Many thinkers who have lost their faith in God tend to give up religion entirely. But Rubenstein sees value in Judaism even without God. Judaism provides the Jew with the deep sense of belonging to a great tradition which brings color, light and warmth into his life and shares its wisdom with him. Consequently Rubenstein says that even though we can no longer believe in God we can believe in the Torah, in Judaism, as a valuable way of life.

Finally, the time of the death of God does not mean the end of all gods. It means the demise of the God who was the ultimate actor in history. I believe in God, the Holy Nothingness known to mystics of all ages, out of which we have come and to which we shall ultimately return. I concur with atheistic existentialists such as Sartre and Camus in much of their analysis of the broken condition of human finitude. We must endure that condition without illusion or hope. I do not part company with them on their analysis of the human predicament. I

part company on the issue of the necessity of religion as the way in which we share that predicament. Their analysis of human hopelessness leads me to look to the religious community as the institution in which that condition can be shared in depth. The limitations of finitude can be overcome only when we return to the Nothingness out of which we have been thrust. In the final analysis, omnipotent Nothingness is Lord of all creation.

Thinkers like Sartre and Camus argue that man really has no hope and he must learn to live with this fact. There is no God and that is all there is to it. To resort to religion is to entertain false hopes. But Rubenstein argues that on the contrary precisely because man is in this condition he needs religion. It enables him to link his lack of hope with others in the same situation and so live with it more adequately. Rubenstein's reference to the mystics is interesting. The Jewish mystics, the Kabbalists, whose views have been discussed in the second volume in this series, sometimes speak of God as Nothing. Very well, says Rubenstein, we shall do the same. If people of like mind will affirm that there is only "Nothing" they will know that they need to huddle together for comfort so that they can find some means of coping with life. In reality, of course, the mystics do not mean to say that there is no God. They mean rather that God is so far above all human understanding that there is nothing in our experience to correspond with Him. He can, therefore, be spoken of as No-thing. The difficulty with Rubenstein's interpretation is that he seems to think of Nothing as an entity. The word nothing, of course, means simply not anything. There cannot be a Nothingness to be "Lord of all creation."

CHAPTER 8

FACKENHEIM: POST-HOLOCAUST JEWISH VALUES

The command to be faithful

How one can believe in God despite the problem of evil.

In the magazine Judaism *(Summer 1967) there appeared a* Symposium *on* Jewish Values in the Post-Holocaust Future. *In the following extract from this Symposium Emil L. Fackenheim discusses the Holocaust, the problems it gives rise to, and his belief that man can still have faith in God. Fackenheim's article can be read, therefore, as a reply to Rubenstein in the previous chapter.*

In the present situation, this question becomes: can we confront the Holocaust, and yet not despair? Not accidentally has it taken twenty years for us to face this question, and it is not certain that we can face it yet. The contradiction is too staggering, and every authentic escape is barred. We are forbidden to turn present and future life into death, as the price of remembering death at Auschwitz. And we are forbidden to affirm present and future life, as the price of forgetting Auschwitz.

Only a completely unfeeling person can allow himself to forget Auschwitz and go on living as if nothing had happened. But we have to go on living as Jews nonetheless. There is therefore a contradiction. Auschwitz seems to prove that all our Jewish living no longer has any meaning. Yet if we go on now, living just the way Jews always used to, that would tend to make us forget Auschwitz

Fackenheim now explores how it is possible both to remember the horrors of Hitler and yet still have faith enough to live Jewishly in the present and for the future.

We have lived in this contradiction for twenty years without being able to face it. Unless I am mistaken, we are now beginning to face it, however fragmentarily and inconclusively. And from this beginning confrontation there emerges what I will boldly term a 614th commandment: *the authentic Jew of today is forbidden to hand Hitler yet another, posthumous victory.* (This formulation is terribly inadequate, yet I am forced to use it until one more adequate is found. First, although no anti-Orthodox implication is intended, as though the 613 commandments stood necessarily in need of change, we must face the fact that something radically new has happened. Second, although the commandment should be positive rather than negative, we must face the fact that Hitler did win at least one victory—the murder of six million Jews. Third, although the very name of Hitler should be erased rather than remembered, we cannot disguise the uniqueness of his evil under a comfortable generality, such as persecution-in-general, tyranny-in-general, or even the-demonic-in-general.)

Orthodoxy speaks of 613 commandments which the Jew has to carry out; 365 are negative commandments—things which one must not *do—and 248 are positive commandments—things one must* do. *Fackenheim here states that the best way of coping with our situation regarding Auschwitz is to say that there is for us, today, a 614th commandment. If Auschwitz, and Hitlerism in general, made the Jew give up his faith, then Hitler would have scored another victory. It is forbidden for Jews to allow Hitler to win. Fackenheim gives three reasons why this is the best way of putting it.*

I think the authentic Jew of today is beginning to hear the 614th commandment. And he hears it whether, as agnostic, he hears no more, or whether, as believer, he hears the voice of the *metzaveh* (the commander) in the *mitzvah* (the commandment). Moreover, it may well be the case that the authentic Jewish agnostic and the authentic Jewish believer are closer today than at any previous time.

A "commandment" in Hebrew is mitzvah. *The one who commands is a* metzaveh. *Fackenheim boldly suggests that Jews who have the courage to live their Jewishness after Auschwitz are really very close to one another whether they call themselves believers or not.*

To be sure, the agnostic hears no more than the *mitzvah*. Yet if he is Jewishly authentic, he cannot but face the fragmentariness of his hearing. He cannot, like agnostics and atheists all around him, regard this *mitzvah* as the product of self-sufficient human reason, realizing itself in an ever-advancing history of autonomous human enlightenment. The 614th commandment must be, to him, an abrupt and absolute *given*, revealed in the midst of total catastrophe.

  On the other hand, the believer, who hears the voice of the *metzaveh* in the *mitzvah*, can hardly hear anything more than the *mitzvah*. The reasons which made Martin Buber speak of an eclipse of God are still compelling. And if, nevertheless, a bond between Israel and the God of Israel can be experienced in the abyss, this can hardly be more than the *mitzvah* itself.

In reality a mitzvah implies that there is a metzaveh. But in our situation even the believer is so disturbed by the terrible question Auschwitz gives rise to that he cannot really hear the voice of the metzaveh i.e., of God. Conversely, the unbeliever as a Jew, and precisely because he refuses to give Hitler the victory, as above, is different from other unbelievers. Mysteriously the mitzvah does beckon him on. What Fackenheim seems to be saying is that the only way Hitler can be denied his victory is for Jews to find their faith again. So, paradoxically, the very magnitude of the evil compels man to face up to the necessity of affirming, despite everything, that there is a God. What moves him to protest with his life against the evil of Hitler, is God. What demands that he affirm that the values the martyrs lived by are real and not simply human impulses, is God.

The implications of even so slender a bond are momentous. If the 614th commandment is binding upon the authentic Jew, then we are, first, commanded to survive as Jews, lest the Jewish people perish. We are commanded, second, to remember in our very guts and bones the martyrs of the Holocaust, lest their memory perish. We are forbidden, thirdly, to deny or despair of God, however much we may have to contend with Him or with belief in Him, lest Judaism perish. We are forbidden, finally, to despair of the world as the place which is to become the kingdom of God, lest we help make it a meaningless place in which God is dead or irrelevant and everything is permitted. To abandon any of these imperatives, in response to Hitler's victory at Auschwitz, would be to hand him yet other, posthumous victories.

How can we possibly obey these imperatives? To do so requires the endurance of intolerable contradictions. Such endurance cannot but bespeak an as yet unutterable faith. If we are capable of this endurance, then the faith implicit in it may well be of historic consequence. At least twice before—at the time of the destruction of the First and of the Second Temples—Jewish endurance in the midst of catastrophe helped transform the world. We cannot know the future, if only because the present is without precedent. But this ignorance on our part can have no effect on our present action. The uncertainty of what will be may not shake our certainty of what we must do.

Note that Fackenheim does not try to give a "reason" why God should have allowed Auschwitz to have happened. He does not want to do this because the evil is so terrible that it becomes offensive to try to explain it away. We do not know why God allowed it to happen. Why not then say simply that there is no God? Fackenheim replies that this would be to give Hitler the victory. But why not give Hitler the victory? Fackenheim would probably reply that all our being cries out against this. Therefore are we not justified in concluding that there is something in the universe which spurs us on this way? Could any proof which swayed our mind be as significant as this feeling we have in our deepest self? If Fackenheim is right, we are on the road to faith in God even though we cannot understand Him fully.

The God who will not die

How a Jew can speak of faith today.

Eugene B. Borowitz is another contemporary liberal Jewish thinker. Like many in his generation, he has found it necessary to reverse the standard question of modern Jewish theology. Instead of asking what modern culture teaches Judaism, he has been inquiring as to what the Jewish tradition, openly confronted, can say to men who live in a sick and troubled civilization. The following selection is taken from Hope Jewish and Hope Secular, *a paper written some months following the Arab-Israeli War of June 1967 and reprinted in* The Future as the Presence of Shared Hope *(ed. Maryellen Muckenhirn, Sheed and Ward, Inc., 1968, pages 104-111).*

It is characteristic of Judaism that if any new statement of atheism was to move the Jewish community since World War II it had to come on the basis of what happened in history rather than because philosophers worry whether statements about God can have significant intellectual content. Jews, for all their intellectuality, do not seem so rationalistic as to consider linguistic problems a compelling reason for saying God is dead. And, in turn, they have been amazed that the major death-of-God thinkers have not discussed the unparalleled destruction of Jews under Hitler as a reason for disbelief in God. That alone has agitated the Jewish community whenever it sought to speak of Jewish faith.

Borowitz refers here to the fact that some thinkers nowadays find difficulties in giving meaning to religious statements so that their

atheism is based on "linguistic problems." This has not bothered Jews
on the whole. What does cause them to doubt is the terrible
destruction of the six million Jews under Hitler.

This social interpretation is, of course, subjective but, I think, quite widespread. Here we come to the problem of how to read the social evidence on an even more significant level. How does one know that this and not that event is revelatory? Why did the Hebrews say it was the Exodus and Sinai and not the 400-year slavery or the Golden Calf that taught them what was finally true and ultimately real? I do not know the answer to these questions. I only know that for me and, I believe, for the Jewish people as a whole the Holocaust was shattering but not determinative. It was not the Sinai of our time. It burned us, tortured us, scarred us, and does so yet today. Nonetheless, its obscene brutality did not become our paradigm for future history. I have never been able to cease wondering, in the technical, Biblical sense, that after the Holocaust there was no mass desertion of Judaism. If anything, there arose in the community as a whole a conscious desire to reclaim and re-establish Jewish existence. It was no more than that. Yet, considering what Jewishness had just entailed, that spontaneous, inner reassertion was uncanny. It testified to that which is more than man's wisdom and courage, which yet sustains and carries him through the terrors of personal and social history.

The Jewish people has spontaneously reacted to Hitler not by mass
desertion but virtually by saying in so many words, although we do
not understand at all why God allowed this to happen we still
believe that Jewish existence is worthwhile.

I find it also, though less significant that today, despite substantial publicity to a community generally recognized as highly secularized, the very few Jewish death-of-God advocates have very little acceptance. I attribute this to the social fact that, while to others to hear of religious atheists sounds new and radical, to us it is somehow very old-fashioned. Atheism is where we all were in the '30s and the '40s, in the days when we still thought university rationalism would redeem the world. That is what those of us who care about Judaism seriously turned away from; to revive it now for a new Judaism seems strangely behind the times. What is more important, the very phenomenon it should explain to us it rather destroys. To say there is no God means that everything is permitted. Now, the Holocaust explained is the Holocaust neutralized. It does not even have a negative power. By what right are we disgusted, nauseated, overwhelmed, outraged, at what happened to the innocent if it was only an honest reflection of reality and not an intolerable violation of a standard of right inherent in the universe itself? The new atheism would rob us of our moral indignation, and it is just that which the Jewish community knows better than to surrender. Some decades back it could be tolerant of an atheism which left ethics standing. Today secular ethics is a vanishing myth, and atheism means nihilism. That is to lose the very moral ground from which the protest against God was launched.

Borowitz here makes the interesting observation that there have been Jewish atheists and secularists long before all the present stress on secularism and yet something so significant has been lacking in the atheistic attitude that Jews today frequently find themselves searching for a deeper understanding of what life is about—and this is in reality a search for God. Our very protest against the evil we have witnessed means that we believe that it is "unnatural," that good is ultimate, and having said that, we are not very far from belief in God.

Post-Holocaust Jewish theology found itself in a period when only a negative methodology might be intellectually bearable, though hardly emotionally effective. Any effort to explain the Holocaust would betray the event and our reactions to it. So, nothing could be said. Yet unbelief was equally impossible, because of the moral affirmation inherent in the very protest. We could not speak, but we could not believe. We could only have a theology of non-non-belief. That was not much, but it was more than nothing. Considering what we had been through, considering that some of us had been through it and refused not to believe, that would until recent days have been the realistic content of Jewish hope.

Note the effective formulation of the present day religious stance "a theology of non-non-belief."

Now, once again, historic events have shaken us to our foundations. One cannot speak of Jewish hope today without discussing the June 1967 Arab-Israeli war — and this within a Biblical frame of reference.

Hope for the individual Jew was until recent times intimately linked with the fate of his people. The individual Jew shares God's Covenant as one of the people of Israel, and this means that he is by divine act tied to all Jews, everywhere in the world, especially those who live in the Land of Israel. This ethnic closeness in a religious faith may be more than what one normally expects in a church, but then God called the Children of Israel to Him as a folk and not as a church. This social structure has over the ages been found fully appropriate to its purpose of endurance through history.

A "church" is basically a group of individuals bound together by ties of religion, but Judaism places a great deal of emphasis rather on the "folk" idea, i.e., the idea of a whole people, bound together by common historical experiences, dedicated to God's service.

Jewish hope, moreover, is linked to what God does in historic time. If the Jews find themselves in a house of bondage, they await God's saving action in the here and now. That was the trauma of the Holocaust. Therefore, if we are to speak of Jewish hope we must speak of the fate of the Jews, and in our times that means, among other communities, quite specifically the State of Israel. That sounds like politics to many Christians and hence strangely unreligious. But Christian categories will not do here. The destiny of the Household of Israel is a theo-political matter now as it was in Biblical times. Neither man's institutions for channeling governmental power nor God's concern with what this people must yet do in history can be eliminated when discussing the Jews and their Judaism.

That Monday afternoon when the war began and no news of what was taking place came through, there was black anxiety throughout the Jewish world. The question was not military: Who would win? It was theological: Would God abandon the people of Israel again and allow the citizens of the State of Israel to be slaughtered by Arab armies? For weeks we had heard Radio Cairo's threats to exterminate the Jews of the State of Israel, and we had watched as the mobs there and in other Arab capitals were whipped into a frenzied hatred of the Israelis. We knew the danger was real and not exaggerated, that if the Arab armies drove back the Israelis there would be an incredible massacre which the Western governments would not intercede in time to stop. And God had shown us already once this century that He could

withdraw from history sufficiently to allow His people to be slaughtered. Could we survive another Holocaust? It was not only the Israeli
armies that were on trial that day but, in very earnest, God Himself.

*Note the very bold but entirely suitable idea in this context that
God Himself was on trial.*

Then came the victory, clean, sharp and decisive; gained by intelligence and skill backed by moral will and determination; unsullied by
brutality, vengefulness, atrocity or vindictiveness. We sophisticates
thought we knew historical reality and, therefore, had discounted
much of the Bible. Now, before our very eyes, history turned Biblical
once again. Of course it was relief, elation, a victory at last, and a
great one. This only begins the explanation, for the truth is that to our
own surprise we sensed the presence of a transcendent reality operat-
ing in history that we had almost come to believe could no longer
make itself felt there. We knew all the technical reasons for the Israeli
success, but we also knew they did not explain what had happened.
Without soldiers and generals, without equipment and training, nothing could have happened; but what happened was more than what
they alone could do, and so we naturally and necessarily gave thanks
to Him who works wonders and delivers His people from Egypt. We
saw Him once again as the God who remembers His Covenant. I am
not saying that the Israeli victory proves to Jews there is a God. I am
saying that what happened in June spoke to us in a way that, for
example, the Sinai campaign of 1956 did not. For a moment the tight,
naturalistic structure through which we secularized men see everything cracked open, and we saw Him. As a result, we cannot speak of
Jewish hope today as we would have done after the Holocaust but
before the war.

You will have noticed that I have not spoken of what happened to
them, there in the State of Israel, but of what happened to *us.* This
was, of course, their politics, their war, and their immediate suffering.
But, while we are not bound to them politically, we were, by virtue
of being one people under God, intimately involved in their crisis.
How could we who have been through this Holocaust and post-Holocaust era together now stand divided in trial or in triumph? Perhaps
neither of us knew how closely we felt tied to them until the moment
of crisis arrived. And it is certain that neither of us realized how deeply

we were still rooted in Jewish tradition until we all stood once again, so unexpectedly, before the Western Wall of the Temple in Old Jerusalem. Irony of ironies, it is that archaic religious symbol which more than anything else explains to agnostics and to religious liberals, to secularists and the non-observant, who the people of Israel is.

Thus in one incredible week we reclaimed two strands of our old Jewish hope: we saw God save our people Israel; and we recognized personally how our individual being was tied to our Covenant folk. And now we could feel free to speak of what had sounded so hollow in the post-Holocaust days, that we, personally and individually, have from time to time felt His helping presence in our lives. In the face of our people's disaster, schooled in secular disbelief, how could we say God still works in human lives and we hope in Him? Now what we have seen broadcast before the entire world makes it possible for us to say in all humility: He has helped us, too. Our experience as a community is once again linked with our individual experience, and the old pattern of Covenant hope on these two levels reasserts itself.

A fruitful discussion on the theme Borowitz alludes to here is what is the meaning of a miracle and how can it be detected.

What we have now regained is not a soothing, easy hope. It encompasses of necessity the reality of pain, even of incredible, inexplicable suffering. It does not relish such experiences nor find them a virtue to be cherished. The suffering of the servant has been foisted on us. Crucifixion is not one of our models. Gladly would we await the Messiah with the normal tests of endurance. Yet in the midst of whatever bondage history may now bring, we can once again hope in His action on our behalf. He did so for our fathers. He did so in our time. We trust He will do so again for our children and our children's children. His Covenant with us remains unbroken.

We do not understand how to explain in technically coherent terms our strange history of service, of suffering, and of continued hope. We know what we have seen gives us no intellectual clarity about the continuing suffering of individual Jews and Jewish communities, of persons and peoples of every faith and none. We still can say nothing about the Holocaust. History is grimmer than we ever imagined and human existence far more difficult than we believed. Still, amidst that very realism, we have a sense of hope. We know that God may try us,

but He does not entirely abandon us. We know our individual existence and social destiny do not escape His saving power. In such a
world as ours that is a lot to know.

*Borowitz issues a warning here. Some religious people have found
so much encouragement as a result of the Israeli victory that they
imagine that faith is now easy. But this is a very superficial view
because there are still many anxieties and tensions and there is still
so much suffering in the world today. What has happened is that we
have seen a glimmer of light in the darkness.*

And knowing that much, must not even we secularized Jews follow
the organic development of Biblical Judaism and move on from personal and social hope to a full-throated eschatological belief? That
surely is incompatible with secularity, but now that we have seen the
secular transcended in our own lives we may find the way to reassert
in our own accents the coming of His Kingdom which will transform
and redeem history. That is more than can be said at present. Indeed,
already the cynics and the sophisticated are eager to analyze away the
religious reality of what we have so freshly gained. I trust that despite
their numbers and their stature they will not succeed but rather that
the promise of the unknown prophet of the Exile will be fulfilled:

> Why sayest thou, O Jacob,
> And speakest, O Israel:
> "My way is hid from the LORD,
> And my right is passed over from my God"?
> Hast thou not known? hast thou not heard
> That the everlasting God, the LORD,
> The Creator of the ends of the earth,
> Fainteth not, neither is weary?
> His discernment is past searching out.
> He giveth power to the faint:
> And to him that hath no might He increaseth strength.
> Even the youths shall faint and be weary,
> And the young men shall utterly fall;
> But they that wait for the LORD shall renew their strength;
> They shall mount up with wings as eagles;
> They shall run, and not be weary;
> They shall walk, and not faint.　　(Isa. 40:27-31)

Torah

THE WORD "Torah" (teaching) originally referred to the Five Books of Moses (the Hebrew word for the Bible is *Tanakh*: *T*orah, *Neviim*-Prophets, and *Ketuvim*-Sacred Writings) and then to the rest of the Bible, to the Rabbinic literature and, indeed, to the whole range of Jewish religious teaching. The traditional belief is that God revealed the Torah to Israel.

This traditional belief has had to face two challenges in modern times; one theoretical, the other practical. Accepting the Bible as revealed truth, accurate in all its details, became difficult when it was realized that the Biblical accounts are not infrequently in conflict with scientific views e.g. on the age of the earth, on the evolution of the human species from lower forms of life, on the sun standing still and revolving round the earth and so on. Moreover Biblical criticism led to conclusions on the dating, authorship and text of the Biblical books at variance with tradition e.g. that parts, at least, of the Five Books of Moses were, in fact, written long after Moses and that the Five Books are not a single document but the result of an editor or editors compiling various sources and working them into a literary unit. On the practical side it had become much more difficult for the Jew desiring to participate to the full in Western life and mix with his non-Jewish friends to be scrupulous in keeping such laws. Moreover the continuing significance of such ritual practices as the dietary laws and the traditional observance of the Sabbath were challenged.

Three attitudes eventually emerged. First, the attitude of Orthodoxy or Neo-Orthodoxy as it is sometimes called. This was that the challenges could be met without the slightest surrender of anything either in traditional thought or traditional observance. At the opposite extreme were those who argued that the traditional view would have to be abandoned, the idea of verbal revelation given up, and with it many specific Jewish practices. Many thinkers, however, have tried to avoid both extremes, accepting that a re-interpretation and re-adjustment of both theory and practice is required but retaining the basic idea of revelation.

The first passage in this section is from the writings of Rabbi Hertz in which he states one of the theoretical problems and suggests a means of coping with it. Herbert Loewe makes an appeal for all the practices of traditional Judaism to be retained, but does so as a highly cultured and educated modern Jew, thoroughly acquainted with the intellectual challenges to faith. Solomon Schechter adopts the middle-of-the-way position to which we have referred. His suggestion that catholic Israel has a decisive vote is important but has been subjected to much criticism chiefly because it is too vague. The famous letter of Franz Rosenzweig shows how it is possible for an observant Jew who believes in the sanctity of the Torah yet to have an open mind on modern Biblical scholarship. Rosenzweig, belonging to an assimilated Jewish family, came to Judaism from without and thus had an appreciation of Judaism's spiritual worth sometimes lacking in those for whom the faith has been familiar from youth. Petuchowski adopts a middle-of-the-way position on Revelation.

But the Torah has a very strong social and ethical content and is concerned with far more than ritual observances. Samson Raphael Hirsch, in the extract quoted, shows how Judaism helps to form the moral character, while Hermann Cohen shows why the prophets were pioneers in the field of social justice. While this aspect was always quite strong in Judaism, it has become a major feature of most modern interpretations of Jewish duty.

Somewhat alike yet fully unique

*How we explain the parallels between Biblical stories
and Babylonian myths.*

*Joseph Herman Hertz (d. 1946) was the Chief Rabbi of Great Britain
and the Commonwealth for over thirty years. His edition of the
Pentateuch (Soncino Press), from which the following is taken
(pages 197-198) is used today all over the English speaking world.
Here he responds to the problem of understanding Torah as divine
revelation when we discover that some of the Torah stories are found
in similar form in other ancient, but non-Hebraic sources. He considers
here the story of the Flood and Noah's Ark and its Babylonian parallel.*

Flood stories are very numerous, and are found in every part of the
world. But these are of little or no interest to the Bible student or to
the modern reader. The Babylonian parallel to the Biblical account
of the Deluge, however, stands in a class by itself. Both the resemblances and the differences of the two accounts are of great importance for the understanding and proper appreciation of the Bible
narrative.

The Babylonian story is as follows: The gods in council decide to
send a Flood upon the earth. One of the gods, Ea, who was present
at the council, resolves to save his favourite Utnapishtim—this is the
name of the Babylonian Noah. He warns him of the impending danger
and at the same time commands him to build a ship. He also furnishes

the 'superlatively clever one', Utnapishtim, with a misleading pretext to offer his contemporaries when questioned as to the reason for building the ship. (In the Rabbinical legend, Noah, during the years of the ship's construction, is a preacher of repentance. 'Turn from your evil ways and live,' is his admonition to his fellow-men). When the ship is built, Utnapishtim fills it with his possessions, his family, dependants, including artisans, together with domestic and wild animals. He then enters it himself and closes the door behind him. The storm rages for six days and nights, till all mankind are destroyed, and the very gods 'cowered in terror like dogs'. On the seventh day, he sends out a dove, which comes back to him. And then he lets go a raven, which does not return. On this, Utnapishtim released all the animals; and leaving the ship, offered a sacrifice. 'The gods gathered like flies over the sacrifice.' The deities then began to quarrel; but eventually Utnapishtim is blessed, and is received into the society of the gods.

The sentence in brackets refers to the way in which the story is treated also in the Rabbinic literature (as Hertz will point out it is also present in the Bible), that it is told in the spirit of sound ethical teaching rather than as a matter of sheer caprice. Utnapishtim does not want anyone else to know what he is doing, but Noah wants everyone to know because he wants people to repent and so avert the Flood. For a comparison between the two versions it is as well to read the Biblical story of the Flood which is found in the Book of Genesis, Chapters 6-8. The Babylonian account is found in the epic poem known as The Gilgamesh Epic. *A useful book which can be consulted is* The Gilgamesh Epic and Old Testament Parallels *by Alexander Heidel, Chicago University Press, in the Phoenix Edition, 1963.*

The resemblances between this Babylonian story and the Biblical account lie on the surface. To mention only a few features common to both: the whole human race is doomed to destruction; one man with his dependants and animals is saved in a ship; the episode of the dove and raven; and after leaving the ship, the man offers sacrifices and receives Divine blessings.

Some modern scholars point out that, in fact, the "ship" is one of the differences, not a point of resemblance. In the Babylonian account the hero is saved in a "ship" but in the Biblical account in an "ark" i.e., a box-like structure, perhaps to suggest total reliance on God rather than on human navigational skill.

Of far greater significance, however, are the differences between the two accounts. The Babylonian story is unethical and polytheistic, devoid of any uniform or exalted purpose, and lacking in reverence and restraint. Not so the terse, direct, and simple Hebrew narrative. Instead of the quarrelsome, deceitful, vindictive pack of Babylonian deities, false to one another and false to men, we have in the Hebrew account the One and Supreme God—holy and righteous in His dealings with man. Unlike its Babylonian counterpart, the Hebrew Deluge is a proclamation of the eternal truth that the basis of human society is justice, and that any society which is devoid of justice deserves to perish, and will inevitably perish. Noah is saved, not through celestial caprice or favouritism, not because he was 'superlatively clever', but because he was righteous and blameless in a perverse generation; a man who was worthy of God's approval, as well as of inaugurating a new era for humanity. An impassable gulf separates the Biblical and the Babylonian Deluge stories. This infinite ethical *difference* between them is recognized even by those who are otherwise hostile to the Bible. 'The Biblical story of the Deluge possesses an intrinsic power to stir the conscience of the world, and it was written with this educational and moral end in view. Of this end there is no trace in the Deluge records outside the Bible' (A. Jeremias).

Thus for Hertz there are parallels between the two accounts but the Biblical account stands out for its profound and eternal moral viewpoint. It is clear from Hertz's writings that he believes, in fact, that the Flood actually happened as related in the Bible. Many modern thinkers would consider the story as "myth" i.e., truth expressed in non-historical story form. They would argue that this is the Hebraic version of a very widespread myth. But they, too, would agree with Hertz that the purpose of those who told it in Israel and their way of telling it was totally different from the other version in that it taught the eternal truth about God and His relationship to man and the way He wishes man to behave.

In its Babylonian form, Assyriologists tell us, the story seems to have been reduced to writing as early as the days of Abraham. It must have been known in substance to the children of Israel in Canaan and later in Egypt. But in the form in which, under God's Providence, the Patriarchs transmitted it to their descendants, it was free from all degrading elements, and became an assertion of the everlasting righteousness of the One God. 'The Babylonian parallel only serves to bring out the unique grandeur of Israel's God-idea, which could thus purify and transform the most uncongenial and repugnant features of the ancient Deluge tradition' (Gunkel).

Although Gunkel was a non-Jewish scholar, Hertz sees no reason not to quote to him even in a commentary to the Torah. It might be useful to quote here Hertz's remarks in his Introduction where he makes this point and also states his complete aversion to Wellhausen: "Jewish and non-Jewish commentators—ancient, medieval, and modern—have been freely drawn upon. 'Accept the truth from whatever source it comes,' is sound Rabbinic doctrine—even if it be from the pages of a devout Christian expositor or of an iconoclastic Bible scholar, Jewish or non-Jewish. This does not affect the Jewish Traditional character of the work. My conviction that the criticism of the Pentateuch associated with the name of Wellhausen is a perversion of history and a desecration of religion, is unshaken; likewise, my refusal to eliminate the Divine either from history or from human life . . ." In the debate on the value of Biblical criticism, Hertz clearly sides with the negative view. Many would agree with Rosenzweig, in the selection that follows, that even if people like Wellhausen were followed, this does not necessarily lead to a "desecration of religion."

The several sources of one revelation

How a modern Jew can honestly believe in the Torah.

*Franz Rosenzweig (1886-1929) is one of the most influential voices
in many a present-day understanding of Judaism. The following letter,
frequently quoted (e.g. in Franz Rosenzweig: His Life and Thought ed.
by Nahum N. Glatzer, Schocken Books Inc., New York, 1953, page 158),
is addressed to Jacob Rosenheim, leader of Orthodoxy in Germany.
The letter is dated April 21, 1927.*

Where we differ from Orthodoxy is in our reluctance to draw from our
belief in the holiness or uniqueness of the Torah, and in its character
of revelation, any conclusions as to its literary genesis and the philo-
logical value of the text as it has come down to us. If all of Wellhausen's theories were correct and the Samaritans really had the
better text, our faith would not be shaken in the least. This is the
profound difference between you and us—a difference which, it seems
to me, may be bridged by mutual esteem but not by understanding. I,
at least, fail to understand the religious basis of Hirsch's commentary
or Breuer's writings. Still, how does it happen then that our translation
is more closely akin to that of Hirsch than to any other? We too trans-
late the Torah as a single book. For us, too, it is the work of one spirit.
Among ourselves we call him by the symbol which critical science is
accustomed to use to designate its assumed redactor: R. But this
symbol R we expand not into Redactor but into *Rabbenu*. For he is
our teacher; his theology is our teaching.

Samson Raphael Hirsch was the famous nineteenth century leader of German Orthodoxy. Isaac Breuer, a prominent Orthodox thinker, was his grandson. The translation to which Rosenzweig refers was one undertaken by him and Martin Buber. Biblical Criticism is divided into the Higher Criticism, which deals with the authorship, background and dating of the Biblical books, and Lower Criticism, which deals with the text of the Bible. Textual Criticism tries to discover whether the text as we have it today is the original one and it uses various ancient versions which frequently have different readings from ours. The most ancient of these versions is that of the Samaritans. Julius Wellhausen (1844-1917) gave the Higher Criticism its fullest exposition. Very briefly stated Wellhausen's view is that the Pentateuch is composed of four distinct "documents." The first of these is called "J" because it uses the special divine of four letters (which in German begins with a J-JHVH). The second uses the divine name Elohim and is therefore called "E." A third source which can be detected is called the "Priestly Document," because it deals chiefly with the priestly functions and was, it is alleged, put together in priestly circles. This is represented by the symbol "P." And finally there is the book of Deuteronomy, which is a separate document, and is represented by the symbol "D." These four separate documents were put together eventually by an editor. The German form for "editor" is Redactor, and his work is represented by the symbol "R." There are thus the four documents of J, E, D and P, made into a unity by R. All this belongs to a past period of Biblical scholarship and nowadays many scholars either reject Wellhausen's views or, at least, modify them. But practically all scholars agree that the Pentateuch is a composite work.

Now obviously this whole approach raises difficulties for traditional Jews who look upon the Torah as divine revelation. The older view was that in the Torah we have the actual words of God and that the text is absolutely accurate in all details. But if Wellhausen is right there is not one Torah at all but a series of documents produced at different ages containing different emphases and even downright contradictions. And if the Samaritans had the better text then we cannot even be sure that we have in our possession the original Torah. Consequently, Orthodoxy, as represented by Hirsch, Breuer and Rosenheim, believes that it is necessary, in the name of faith, to reject all untraditional theories such as those of Wellhausen and to deny that any of the ancient versions can ever be right when it conflicts with the text we now have. Others who followed Wellhausen were prepared to give up the whole concept of revelation. Rosenzweig differs from both these schools.

Rosenzweig's position is that even if Wellhausen is right and even if the Samaritans had the better text (he does not say that this is, in fact, so but that we must be prepared to face the possibility) our present text was put together under God's guidance. The "Redactor" was inspired by God to put the whole together in this way rather than in any other and this book in this form became Israel's Torah. Therefore, says Rosenzweig, we continue to use the symbol "R" but for us it does not stand for "Redactor" but for Rabbenu, which means "our teacher." He is our teacher who has conveyed to us the book that has been most instrumental in the formation of the Jewish spirit. This is a nice play on words. Moses is often called Moshe Rabbenu, Moses our teacher. So even if the Torah is not by Moses, it is still by Rabbenu. What Rosenzweig is saying is that if we wish to know how the various parts of the Torah came to be we must go to Biblical scholarship, and here we must be prepared to examine all the evidence with complete honesty. If we come to the conclusion that Wellhausen is right, we must accept his findings. But the process as a whole also has to be understood. The Jew who has faith will not fail to see the hand of God in this process as a whole i.e. through the work of people like the Redactor-Rabbenu. This approach bears strong affinities to that of Schechter, which we shall be reading.

Rosenzweig also says that on the intellectual plane there can be no compatibility between him and Hirsch. He is prepared to accept untraditional theories as to authorship and Hirsch believes this to be a betrayal of the Torah. But strangely enough if there is mutual esteem, both views can be seen as arriving at the same Torah. Rosenzweig, in fact, points out to Rosenheim that both he and Hirsch remarkably hit upon the same meaning of the Torah for Jews today. This is not surprising since whether, as Hirsch argues, the Torah was given in this form to Moses or whether, as Rosenzweig is prepared to accept, it grew gradually over the ages, the final result is the same for both. For both of them the Torah we now have is the Torah.

Age may well mean wisdom

The relevance of keeping the old laws.

*Herbert Loewe (1882-1940) was a lecturer in Semitics at both Oxford
and Cambridge and a great Jewish influence on Jewish undergraduates
at the universities. The following selection from his pamphlet*
The Orthodox Position *(Cambridge, 1915, pages 13-19) is the
statement of a highly cultured Orthodox Jew.*

The number of the Mosaic precepts for which we cannot see the reason
is small: most of them were connected with the Temple and Palestine
and are no longer binding. Far more "faith-disturbing", so to speak,
to some of our brethren, are certain of the *Mitzvoth* which ought, they
consider, to be superseded. It has been said that the Almighty does not
take pleasure in them, no longer commands their practice, that they are
at best, obsolete; at worst, superstitions and impediments. "What is the
good of wearing *Tzitzith*? What is the harm in eating shrimps?"

Well, Orthodox Judaism regards all these things as divinely ordained,
as necessary, and as irremovable. Now neither we, nor those who differ
from us, claim any monopoly either of knowledge and critical faculties
or of mental honesty. We and they alike can think out problems, can
see difficulties and face them, can entertain doubts and struggle to
faith. Honesty of purpose is not confined to one sect. Nor had our
teachers any material interests for the sake of which they might have
been tempted to suppress the truth. For centuries our Rabbis earned

their living by duties in other professions—their religious work was unpaid. Consequently their thoughts were completely independent. Every age has brought fresh questions for Judaism to face, it has had to adjust itself to every new scientific discovery. That our Rabbis — men of learning and probity — should regularly have maintained that there is a moral value in not eating shrimps and in wearing Tzitzith, is a convincing argument that we are not acting blindly, nor without due reflection. There must be something in these things, or else thinking generations would not have agreed upon their retention. When, then, we rely on the decision of the past, we need fear neither interested bias nor obscurantism.

Tzitzit are the fringes worn on the "corners of the garment" (see Numbers 15:37-41), nowadays attached to the Tallit, the prayershawl worn in the Synagogue, and also to a special small square worn for that purpose by Orthodox Jews. Shrimps are forbidden according to Leviticus, Chapter 11. Mitzvot means "commandments." Loewe argues that apart from other considerations a good reason for keeping these laws is that great teachers of the past considered them necessary and of moral value. He then goes on to consider how these are of value.

The next answer is that all these *Mitzvoth* are necessary to establish and maintain Jewish life in its perfection. Every secular act of the Orthodox Jew is invested with some reminder, some association with religion in order to consecrate his whole life. Every emotion, every phase of the soul and body, is taken into account, "When we lie down, and when we rise up." Daily prayer, Sabbatical rest, festival joys, penitential solemnity, mourning in Ab, merriment at Purim; these are a few of the characteristics. Who can know the Jewish life save the Jew? Every Sabbath is a family feast, a day of prayer, of rest, of study, of good cheer. The year is a series of events, as artistically perfect as a Wagnerian cycle. Take, for example, the period from the first solemn call to repentance on the Sabbath eve, when the penitential season opens, until after *Sukkoth*, the gaiety dies away peacefully on Sabbath Bereshith, a sober prelude to the coming of winter. In this period how wonderfully does each day fit into the general scheme, how the note of penitence rises in intensity until the consciousness of full pardon is reached in the grand diapason of Kippur, how the relief from the burden of sin gives way to rejoicing, until Tabernacles ends in the merry-making of Simchath Torah and the lengthening evenings invite us to recommence our study of the Law. Just as each sentiment, during these great days, has its musical "Leitmotif" — its canonical colour, so to speak — so is the whole range of human feeling covered by the complex body of customs, precepts, prayers and poems which make up what we call the Jewish Life. The value of this life has never been questioned. It has preserved Jewry and Judaism throughout the ages amid the cramping walls of Ghettos and slums. It has created Jewish family life with its virtues of chastity, charity, love and righteousness, nowhere surpassed, and rarely equalled. For all this is simply due to the *Mitzvoth*, by which, if a man do them, he shall live. The *Mitzvoth* are the abiding proof that it is not by bread alone that man lives. Nothing is "trivial". Life is made up of the "common round and trivial task", which the *Mitzvah* brightens and hallows.

Loewe posits that the whole round of Jewish duty—the Mitzvot—is like a great musical symphony, every note of which is significant and none is trivial. Seen in isolation some things are indeed petty and insignificant. However, they should not be seen in isolation but all as part of a tremendous whole, the aim of which is to bring religion and moral worth into the whole of life. He then goes on to say that it all depends on how one looks at these things. He refers to the vision of the "dry bones" (Ezekiel, Chapter 37). The ordinary Babylonian (Ezekiel lived in Babylon) saw simply dry bones but the prophet saw much deeper.

The Babylonian, standing in the valley, saw but a heap of dry bones. The Prophet discerned the reviving spirit of God; the "trivial" *Mitzvoth*, like the dry bones are "all the house of Israel". These *Mitzvoth* cannot possibly be separated or differentiated. No one, say the Rabbis, can know the relative worth of them. No sooner does a Jew begin to discriminate, than decay sets in. Each individual *Mitzvah* represents a separate but integral brick in a building. Everyone who starts whittling away will ultimately lose all. There is only one logical conclusion to the whittling process, and that is the Christian one. Either *all* of the *Mitzvoth* or none. If you believe in the founder of Christianity, you do not need the *Mitzvoth;* that is Christian doctrine. The converse is true in the case of Judaism, but the converse means EVERY *Mitzvah*.

It is quite true that any given man may succeed in making a selection, but the result is inevitably that his children will make a further selection — not from the whole, but from the father's part. This is why the wearing of fringes and the abstaining from shrimps must be retained. Our children will not begin where we began, but where we end. Once we make a start, we can forsee neither the lengths to which we shall be driven nor the rapidity of our progress. From Orthodox Judaism, once the "fence" is gone, to simple Theism, the step is short.

Loewe uses the argument that to whittle away even the smallest thing will be the "thin end of the wedge" and all that will be left will be a simple belief in God (simple Theism) without any of the riches of Judaism to which he has previously called attention. The Rabbis speak of things not wrong in themselves but forbidden as a means of protecting Judaism, a "fence" to the Torah. Hence, Loewe says that to give up any of the Mitzvot is to make a breach in the fence and eventually the whole will collapse. There follows an example Loewe gives of the rapid movement from some minor changes to a complete abandonment in some circles of most of the Jewish practices which took place in some sections of Reform Judaism. For reasons of space this passage has been omitted. A number of other paragraphs have been omitted for the same reason and we now take up the argument as it appears on page 18.

"But what about Progress? Has not human nature developed?" Certainly, the prophet who became conscious that he was no better than his fathers, asked for instant death, and the divine reply showed that his premises were false. But, first of all, the sanction of age is strong: it cannot be broken without very great cause. Religious — or, if you prefer it, national — pride must make us attached to old customs. One of the most surprising results of the most recent review of the Code of Hammurabi has been the discovery that these ancient Babylonian laws have more affinity with Rabbinic than with Pentateuchal Judaism. When then our *dinim* and *minhagim* go back, some of them, to the earliest dawn of history, shall we let them lapse while remaining faithful to others of modern date that we have adopted in England? Shall we then go to the stake for ceremonies like the Lord Mayor's show, or the picturesque — but alas! expensive — function of taking a Degree, or the gorgeous displays of a Coronation, the peculiar customs of a regiment or a college, and at the same time be indifferent to our own usages, immeasurably older and more precious? To observe the time-honoured manner of celebrating the 1st of January by singing Auld Lang Syne with one foot on the table, is no doubt an excellent thing. Is it then less excellent to celebrate the 1st of Tishri by eating apple and honey? Is a Christmas tree more significant, more elevating, more interesting archaeologically or historically than a Hanuca lamp? Are "Haman's ears" less tasty than plum pudding? It is sad to see people blind to our own beautiful customs while eager to observe punctiliously the social habits of our Gentile friends. It is not only sad, but ludicrous; and our friends — and enemies — think so too. Our Jewish Scottish lairds in their tartan, our ostentatious marranos who are ashamed of their religious duties — these afford copy to the comic papers and bring discredit on us. But who ever saw a skit on a *Bethhammidrash* or a caricature of a Rabbi? What Christian writer has ever made fun of a *Sefer Torah*, a *Shofar* or *Matzoth*? It is we alone who mock at or belittle these things.

The reference to the prophet is to Elijah in the book of Kings (I Kings, 19:4-8). Loewe says that the Code of Hammurabi, one of the earliest Codes in human history, predating the Pentateuch, contains laws which are closer to those found in the Rabbinic literature than in the Pentateuch. This can only mean that many of the laws found among the Rabbis are very ancient usages which came down to them by tradition. If, then, he argues, a man has any feeling for tradition he ought to respect such ancient laws and customs. The argument in this section will not appeal to every type of mind. Some might feel that it is wrong to attach quite so much importance to tradition and will look elsewhere for a justification of the Jewish laws, as, indeed, Loewe himself does in this essay. Dinim are laws, minhagim are customs. On the 1st of Tishri, the Jewish New Year, it is customary to eat an apple dipped in honey as a symbol of sweetness in the year ahead. "Haman's ears" are, of course, the pies or cakes eaten on the festival of Purim—hamantaschen. The marranos were the Jews in the time of the Inquisition who were forced to hide their Jewishness, though they kept the Jewish law in private. Loewe calls modern Jews who are ashamed of their own religious practices but only too ready to adopt the customs of their Gentile friends "ostentatious marranos." A Bet Ha-Midrash, House of Learning, is a place in which the Torah is studied.

The community as our guide

Who decides the correct Jewish way of life.

Solomon Schechter (1849-1915), President of the Jewish Theological Seminary of America, was a founder of Conservative Judaism. The following selection is from his Studies in Judaism (The Jewish Publication Society of America, Philadelphia, 1945, Introduction, pages 10-17). In it Schechter develops his idea of "Catholic Israel."

Some years ago when the waves of the Higher Criticism of the Old Testament reached the shores of this country, and such questions as the heterogeneous composition of the Pentateuch, the comparatively late date of the Levitical Legislation, and the post-exilic origin of certain Prophecies as well as of the Psalms began to be freely discussed by the press and even in the pulpit, the invidious remark was often made: What will now become of Judaism when its last stronghold, the Law, is being shaken to its very foundations?

Such a remark shows a very superficial acquaintance with the nature of an old historical religion like Judaism, and the richness of the resources it has to fall back upon in cases of emergency.

The Higher Criticism is the study of the Bible with an attempt to discover as accurately as possible the answers to such questions as the date and background of the Biblical books. Among the conclusions that many scholars came to was that the Pentateuch (the Five Books of Moses), traditionally said to have been written down by Moses

71

at the command of God, was not in large part written by Moses at all but was a work composed of different strands produced at different periods in Israel's history and that some parts of it (e.g. the laws in Leviticus) were very much later than Moses. It was also held that some of the Prophecies were not written by the prophets whose names they bear and some of the Psalms were not written by King David but were written after the period of the Babylonian exile. On the face of it such views seemed very harmful to Judaism, which is based on the Bible, particularly the Pentateuch. But, says Schechter, Judaism is an historical religion — it has had a very long history and is capable of meeting such challenges in the present as it has done in the past. What he is leading up to is the view that the real source of authority in Judaism is not, in fact, the Bible but the Bible as interpreted in Jewish life and history.

As a fact, the emergency did not quite surprise Judaism. The alarm signal was given some one hundred and fifty years ago by an Italian Rabbi, Abiad Sar Shalom Bazilai, in his pamphlet *The Faith of the Sages.* The pamphlet is, as the title indicates, of a polemical character, reviewing the work of the Jewish rationalistic schools; and after warming up in his attacks against their heterodox views, Bazilai exclaims: "Nature and simple meaning, they are our misfortune." By "nature and simple meaning" Bazilai, who wrote in Hebrew, understood what we would call Natural Science and Philology. With the right instinct of faith, Bazilai hit on the real sore points. For though he mostly argues against the philosophical systems of Aristotle and his commentators, he felt that it is not speculation that will ever seriously endanger religion. There is hardly any metaphysical system, old or new, which has not in course of time been adapted by able dialecticians to the creed which they happened to hold. In our own time we have seen the glorious, though not entirely novel spectacle, of Agnosticism itself becoming the rightful handmaid of Queen Theology. The real danger lies in "nature" (or Natural Science) with its stern demand of law and regularity in all phenomena, and in the "simple meaning" (or Philology) with its inconsiderate insistence on truth. Of the two, the "simple meaning" is the more objectionable. Not only is it very often at variance with Tradition, which has its own code of interpretation, but it is constantly increasing the difficulties raised by science. For if words could only have more than one meaning, there would be no objection to reading the first words of Genesis, "In a beginning God *evolved.*" The difficulties of science would then be disposed of easily enough. Maimonides, who was as bold an interpreter as he was a deep metaphysician, hinted plainly enough that were he as convinced of the eternity of matter as he was satisfied of the impossibility of any corporeal quality in the deity, he would feel as little compunction in explaining (figuratively) the contents of the first chapter of Genesis as he did in allegorising the anthropomorphic passages of the Bible. Thus in the end all the difficulties resolve themselves into the one great difficulty of the "simple meaning." The best way to meet this difficulty was found to be to shift the centre of gravity in Judaism and to place it in the secondary meaning, thus making religion independent of philology and all its dangerous consequences.

If words can mean anything one chooses to make them mean there can be no conflict between modern science and the plain Biblical meaning because one could give the Bible whatever meaning one chooses. In the Middle Ages this is precisely what many thinkers did. But nowadays we are too much aware of philology, of the science of word meaning, to permit ourselves to adopt this way out of the difficulty. We are obliged to say that the plain meaning of the Bible, the "simple meaning," cannot possibly be squared with science. But in that case what becomes of our religion? Schechter replies that in addition to the "plain" or "simple" meaning, there has grown up a "secondary" meaning i.e., the meaning of the Bible as it became interpreted in later Jewish thought. This is certainly not the "plain" meaning and we have to acknowledge this so that if our center of gravity were in the meaning of the Bible itself we would, indeed, be in trouble. But what is required is to shift the center of gravity from the plain to the secondary meaning. This suggests that the real authority for Judaism is not in the Bible at all but in the living tradition of interpretation and re-interpretation. Consequently, this interpretative process can still be carried out and we, in our turn, can re-interpret Judaism so that it does not conflict with our present-day knowledge.

This shifting work was chiefly done, perhaps not quite consciously, by the historical school which followed upon that of Mendelssohn and his first successors. The historical school, which is still in the ascendant, comprises many of the best Jewish writers who either by their learning or by their ecclesiastical profession as Rabbis and preachers in great communities have acquired some important position among their brethren. The men who have inaugurated this movement were Krochmal (1785-1840), Rapoport (1790-1867), and Zunz (1794-1886).

Moses Mendelssohn, at the end of the eighteenth century, was, it has been said, the first "modern" Jew i.e. the first to consider seriously the problems of the Jews in the Western World.
His immediate followers were called the Maskilim, "Enlightened."
After them arose in Germany and Galicia the movement founded by the scholars Schechter mentions. This became known as the "historical school," the school which studied in great detail the history of the Jews in order to discover what actually had happened in the past. The movement is also known as that of Jüdische Wissenschaft, "The Science of Judaism."

It is not a mere coincidence that the first representatives of the historical school were also the first Jewish scholars who proved themselves more or less ready to join the modern school of Bible Criticism, and even to contribute their share to it. The first two, Krochmal and Rapoport, early in the second quarter of this century accepted and defended the modern view about a second Isaiah, the post-exilic origin of many Psalms, and the late date of Ecclesiastes; whilst Zunz, who began (in 1832) with denying the authenticity of Ezekiel; concluded his literary career (1873) with a study on the Bible (*Gesammelte Schriften, i,* pp. 217-290), in which he expressed his view "that the Book of Leviticus dates from a later period than the Book of Deuteronomy, later even than Ezekiel, having been composed during the age of the Second Temple, when there already existed a well-established priesthood which superintended the sacrificial worship." But when Revelation or the Written Word is reduced to the level of history, there is no difficulty in elevating history in its aspect of Tradition to the rank of Scripture, for both have then the same human or divine origin (according to the student's predilection for the one or the other adjective), and emanate from the same authority. Tradition becomes thus the means whereby the modern divine seeks to compensate himself for the loss of the Bible, and the theological balance is to the satisfaction of all parties happily readjusted.

When Schechter refers to "this century" he means the last century,
at the end of which he wrote this essay. His chief point here is
that it had been a habit to look at the Bible as a kind of magical book
unaffected by history at all, dropping down, as it were, directly
from heaven. The historical school shows that this is not so and that
the Biblical text had a long history. But once history is invoked then
Tradition, too, has a history. Consequently, if the believer looks at
the whole process he will see both the Bible and the way it was
interpreted in Jewish tradition as "divine" i.e., he will see this as the
way God is leading His people. The unbeliever will see it all as
human, but then, he would, in any event, see the Bible in this way too.
It follows that although from one point of view the Bible is now
"lost" i.e., the human element is seen in it, from another point of
view we now have Tradition.

Jewish Tradition, or, as it is commonly called, the Oral Law, or, as we may term it (in consideration of its claims to represent an interpretation of the Bible), the Secondary Meaning of the Scriptures, is mainly embodied in the works of the Rabbis and their subsequent followers during the Middle Ages. Hence the zeal and energy with which the historical school applied itself to the Jewish post-biblical literature, not only elucidating its texts by means of new critical editions, dictionaries, and commentaries, but also trying to trace its origins and to pursue its history through its gradual development. To the work of Krochmal in this direction a special essay is devoted in this volume. The labours of Rapoport are more of a biographical and bibliographical nature, being occupied mostly with the minor details in the lives and writings of various famous Jewish Rabbis in the Middle Ages; thus they offer but little opportunity for general theological comment. Of more importance in this respect are the hints thrown out in his various works by Zunz, who was just as emphatic in asserting the claims of Tradition as he was advanced in his views on Bible criticism. Zunz's greatest work is *Die Gottesdienstliche Vorträge*—an awkward title, which in fact means "The History of the Interpretation of the Scriptures as forming a part of the divine service." Now if a work displaying such wide learning and critical acumen and written in such an impartial spirit can be said to have a bias, it was towards bridging over the seemingly wide gap between the Written Word (the Scriptures) and the Spoken Word (the Oral Law or Tradition), which was the more deeply felt, as most of Zunz's older contemporaries were men, grown up in the habits of thought of the eighteenth century— a century distinguished both for its ignorance of, and its power of ignoring, the teachings of history. Indeed it would seem that ages employed in making history have no time for studying it.

The Rabbis speak of two Torot: *the Written Law and the Oral Law. Schechter elaborates on the thought that this does not mean simply that side by side with the written word of Scripture there was an oral tradition, handed down from generation to generation which explained it. The doctrine of the Oral Law, as understood by Zunz and the others Schechter mentions, is a much richer concept. It means that the written word of Scripture was constantly finding new forms of expression throughout the varying history of the Jews and it is this dynamic tradition that it referred to as the Oral Law.*

Zunz accomplished the task he set himself, by showing, as already indicated, the late date of certain portions of the Bible, which by setting the early history of Israel in an ideal light betray the moralising tendency of their authors, and are, in fact, little more than a traditional interpretation of older portions of Scripture, adapted to the religious needs of the time. Placing thus the origin of Tradition in the Bible itself, it was a comparatively easy matter for Zunz to prove its further continuity. Prophecy and Interpretation are with him the natural expressions of the religious life of the nation; and though by the loss of Israel's political independence the voice of the prophets gradually died away, the voice of God was still heard. Israel continues to consult God through the medium of the Scriptures, and He answers His people by the mouth of the Scribes, the Sages, the Interpreters of the Law; whilst the liturgy of the Synagogue, springing up at the time when Psalms were still being composed, expands in its later stages through the work of the Poets of the Synagogue into such a rich luxuriance "that it forms in itself a treasure of history, poetry philosophy; and prophecy and psalms are again revived in the hymnology of the Middle Ages." This is in brief the lesson to be learned from Zunz's *Gottesdienstliche Vorträge* as far as it deals with the significance of Tradition; and it is in the introduction to this work that Zunz expresses himself to the following effect: Indispensable is the free Spoken Word. Mankind has acquired all its ideal treasures only by Word of Mouth; an

education continuing through all stages of life. In Israel, too, the Word of Instruction transmitted from mouth to mouth was never silenced.

The quote is from Zunz. Schechter here paraphrases Zunz. It is a mistake to look upon Scripture and Tradition as two entirely distinct entities. The aspects of Tradition, in which earlier teachings are re-interpreted, are found in Scripture itself, where, sometimes, an old tale is retold in a more ideal fashion as a lesson for the present. On the other hand, the kind of activity for which the prophet was noted and the psalmist continued, is, in a sense, in the post-Biblical literature. So there is a living tradition. A mere Written Text is dead. Written in a previous generation it has in itself no power to speak to a later generation. But when a living tradition is constantly re-interpreting a written text, that text is always fresh and alive.

The historical school has never, to my knowledge, offered to the world a theological programme of its own. By the nature of its task, its labours are mostly conducted in the field of philology and archaeology, and it pays but little attention to purely dogmatic questions. On the whole, its attitude towards religion may be defined as an enlightened Scepticism combined with a staunch conservatism which is not even wholly devoid of a certain mystical touch. As far as we may gather from vague remarks and hints thrown out now and then, its theological position may perhaps be thus defined:—It is not the mere revealed Bible that is of first importance to the Jew, but the Bible as it repeats itself in history, in other words, as it is interpreted by Tradition. The Talmud, that wonderful mine of religious ideas from which it would be just as easy to draw up a manual for the most orthodox as to extract a vade-mecum for the most sceptical, lends some countenance to this view by certain controversial passages—not to be taken seriously—in which "the words of the scribes" are placed almost above the words of the Torah. Since then the interpretation of Scripture or the Secondary Meaning is mainly a product of changing historical influences, it follows that the centre of authority is actually removed from the Bible and placed in some *living body,* which, by reason of its being in touch with the ideal aspirations and the religious needs of the age, is best able to determine the nature of the Secondary Meaning. This living body, however, is not represented by any section of the nation, or any corporate priesthood, or Rabbihood, but by the collective conscience of Catholic Israel as embodied in the Universal Synagogue. The Synagogue "with its long, continuous cry after God for more than twenty-three centuries," with its unremittent activity in teaching and developing the Word of God, with its uninterrupted succession of prophets, Psalmists, Scribes, Assideans, Rabbis, Patriarchs, Interpreters, Elucidators, Eminences, and Teachers, with its glorious record of Saints, martyrs, sages, philosophers, scholars, and mystics; this Synagogue, the only true witness to the past, and forming in all ages the sublimest expression of Israel's religious life, must also retain its authority as the sole true guide for the present and the future. And being in communion with this Synagogue, we may also look hopefully for a safe and rational solution of our present theological troubles. For was it not the Synagogue which even in antiquity determined the fate of Scripture? On the one hand, for example, books like Ezekiel, the Song of Songs, and Ecclesiastes, were only declared to be Holy Writ in virtue of the interpretation put upon them by the Rabbis: and, on the other hand, it was the veto of the Rabbis which excluded from the canon the works that now pass under the name of Apocrypha. We may, therefore, safely trust that the Synagogue will again assert its divine right in passing judgment upon the Bible when it feels called upon to exercise that holy office. It is "God who has chosen the Torah, and Moses His servant, and Israel His people." But indeed God's choice invariably coincides with the wishes of Israel; He "performeth all things" upon which the councils of Israel, meeting under promise of the Divine presence and communion, have previously agreed. As the Talmud somewhere expresses itself with regard to the Book of Esther, "They have confirmed above what Israel has accepted below."

What Schechter is saying here can perhaps be best understood on the analogy of the Catholic Church. For the devout Catholic it is not the Bible that is the real source of religious authority but the Church. The important difference, however, is that in Catholicism the Church means chiefly the Pope, Cardinals and Bishops, but in Judaism there is no priesthood of this kind and it is the people as a whole, its teachers and sages drawn from every class, who work out, as it were, in each generation what the Torah is. Two strong objections have been made to Schechter's whole approach. First, in the light of so much difference of opinion among Jews today, where is the voice of Catholic Israel to be heard? Which group can claim to speak for Catholic Israel? Second, what would happen, for example, if the majority of Jews decided not to keep the Sabbath? Would that mean that the voice of Catholic Israel speaks for the right to abandon the Sabbath? Such a view would be ridiculous, but does it not follow from Schechter's presentation? As someone has put it, in the days of Elijah, when all Israel went after Baal, does this mean that Baal worship was right because Catholic Israel was in its favor?

Another consequence of this conception of Tradition is that it is neither Scripture nor primitive Judaism, but general custom which forms the real rule of practice. Holy Writ as well as history, Zunz tells us, teaches that the law of Moses was never fully and absolutely put in practice. Liberty was always given to the great teachers of every generation to make modifications and innovations in harmony with the spirit of existing institutions. Hence a return to Mosaism would be illegal, pernicious, and indeed impossible. The norm as well as the sanction of Judaism is the practice actually in vogue. Its consecration is the consecration of general use—or, in other words, of Catholic Israel. It was probably with a view to this communion that the later mystics introduced a short prayer to be said before the performance of any religious ceremony, in which, among other things, the speaker professes his readiness to act "in the name of all Israel."

The Ḥanukkah lights, for example, are not mentioned in the Bible at all. They hardly could be since the events they commemorate took place long after the Biblical period. To take another example, the Synagogue and its prayers are post-Biblical. Yet they are certainly an important part of Judaism because this is how Judaism has developed. This is how God, as it were, has commanded His will through the historical experiences of Catholic Israel.

Meaning and origin

On whether a modern Jew should keep practices
which have a pagan origin.

Jakob J. Petuchowski (b. 1925) is a Professor at the Hebrew Union
College-Jewish Institute of Religion, Cincinnati, and a leading Reform
thinker. The following extract is from his book Ever Since Sinai: A
Modern View of Torah *(Scribe Publications Inc., New York, 1961,*
pages 74-83). Petuchowski has considered the meaning of the ethical
commands of the Torah. He here goes on to consider the rituals of
the Torah in the light of our present-day knowledge. Detailed
comment to this section is not required because Petuchowski writes
very clearly and explains himself most adequately.

So far we have been considering one type of Torah law only—the
moral and ethical kind. But, as is well-known, a great part of the
legislation of the Torah deals with those acts which are commonly
described as "ritual" or "ceremonial." How do they fit into the picture of Revelation? Let us take as our first illustration the laws governing the Passover. The Israelites, as was already mentioned, experienced God as the "Author of Liberty." Their liberation from
Egyptian slavery was understood by them as an expression of God's
Will that man must be free. Their own experience of this liberation
left an indelible mark on their souls. But how could they transmit this
"mark" to their children and their children's children? How could

they enable future generations to *re-live* the events of the Exodus? For "re-lived" they must be—both by the complacent Jew, living in freedom, who must be reminded of tasks yet to be accomplished, and by the suffering Jew, in persecution, who must be strengthened in his hope for redemption.

The answer was provided by the detailed provisions of the Passover observance. We eat the kind of unleavened bread they ate. We partake of bitter herbs to remind ourselves of the bitterness of their lives. And we celebrate the *seder* night, thus annually re-living the moment of their liberation. As the Passover Haggadah puts it: "In every generation each Jew must regard himself as though he, too, had been liberated from Egypt." And by regarding ourselves in this light, by celebrating the Passover, we never allow ourselves to forget that the God we worship is the "Author of Liberty," Who wants man to be free. Consequently, all the laws and regulations pertaining to our observance of Passover can be said to be "divine laws."

In this connection it should be emphasized that, for an observance to be a part of the "divine Law," it does not mean that the observance cannot have antedated its incorporation into the Torah. For example, modern scholars are of the opinion that the eating of unleavened bread was an important part of the spring festival celebrated by the pagan Canaanite farmers long before Israel entered Palestine. Yet, what makes an observance part of the Torah is not at all the meaning and significance which this observance may *originally* have had in a pagan environment, but the meaning *given to it* within the framework of the Torah. Maimonides already recognized that this was the yardstick to be applied to the whole sacrificial legislation of the Torah, in which he saw an *adaptation* of pagan methods of worship to the requirements of Israel's monotheistic faith. And even Maimonides merely elaborated a point of view expressed long before him in the Midrash.

Fascinated as we might well be by archaeological researches into Hebrew antiquities, we must be on our guard against committing, what a modern philosopher of religion has called, the "Fallacy of Primitivism." This fallacy is committed by the person who is so obsessed with beginnings that he supposes the first stage of the development of any process to reveal what the process really is. Guarding against this "Fallacy of Primitivism," the believing Jew today sees no need to deny, on dogmatic grounds, that the sabbath may have originated in Babylonia, or that the dietary laws may go back to primitive food taboos. What matters to him is the social and religious meaning given to the *biblical* sabbath, and the admonition to holiness and self-discipline which introduces the listing of the *biblical* dietary laws. Such observances, to conclude, are not part of the "divine Law" because they are *"Jewish* inventions," but because they are made to serve a purpose within the Torah's own frame of reference. It is precisely in the hallowing of the ordinary and the customary that the genius of the Torah becomes apparent.

This approach should be compared with that of Rosenzweig and Schechter. The dietary laws are a good example of the different attitudes on revelation. The Orthodox view, as represented by Hirsch, for example, would feel obliged to deny that these laws ever had their origin in primitive food taboos. Some Reform thinkers would argue that since they did have their origin in such taboos they no longer are binding because we have no use today for primitive taboos. Those who agree with Petuchowski agree with the Reform on the question of origins, but with the Orthodox on whether the practices are binding. In Petuchowski's thinking they are binding because of what the Bible makes of them: the sanctifying of every day pursuits such as eating and drinking.

We have taken the Passover observances as an illustration of the "ritual" or "ceremonial" type of legislation. Though a very familiar illustration, it is, however, not an example of the purely "ritual." The "message" of the Passover does, after all, point to the social and ethical realm. There are, on the other hand, many laws of the Torah which are "ritual" pure and simple—without any apparent relation to man's moral duties. Here we are thinking of the elaborate sacrificial cult, of the whole realm of levitical purity, and of the many minutiae regulating worship. How could such observances ever have been presented as the "laws of God"?

The answer is not difficult at all. We have seen that Revelation is a manifestation, a *mysterious* manifestation, of the Love of God. It affects levels of man's being far below the conscious one of his rationalty—as indeed all love does. And man wants to hang on to this experience. He wants to re-live it again and again. And, therefore, he tries to create the circumstances which seem to be the most propitious, which seem to have "worked" in the past. In places where God has revealed Himself in the past, it is natural for man to erect temples and sanctuaries—in the hope of experiencing there future divine manifestations. And it is the love for God, too, which impels a man to elaborate such acts as are understood to be the manner of worshipping Him.

"This is my God, and I will glorify Him," we read in Exodus 15:2. But the Hebrew word, here translated "glorify," really means "beautify." This elicits the question of Rabbi Ishmael: "But is it possible for a man of flesh and blood to beautify his Creator?!" And he answers that the word must be understood as follows: "I shall be beautiful before Him in observing the commandments. I shall prepare before Him a beautiful *lulav*, a beautiful *sukkah*, beautiful fringes, and beautiful phylacteries." On the other hand, Abba Saul, reading the word under discussion *(anvehu)* as *ani vehu* ("I and He"), interprets: "O be like unto Him! Just as He is gracious and merciful, so be thou also gracious and merciful."

Petuchowski understands the meaning of the purely ritual commandments as establishing a relationship between God and man. They are not purely rational, but then love is not purely rational. One can think, for example, of a couple in love playing over and over a recording of the tune they heard when they first met because this awakens precious memories and binds them closer together. This approach should be compared with Buber's remarks on I and Thou as above. Rabbi Ishmael and Abba Saul were Rabbis who lived in Palestine in the second century.

It is interesting to note that here both the "ritual" and the "ethical" are linked to one and the same biblical passage. But this is exactly how the Jew reacts to the Love of God, how he, as it were, returns it on both the "ethical" and the "ritual" level. And, since the same impulse that is behind the one is also behind the other, the laws which fence in the two levels are, with the same logic, traced back to the same Divine Revelation, the same "giving of the Torah." There is, however, as both Buber and Rosenzweig have taught us, an important distinction which must be drawn between "legislation" and "commandment." Legislation is "on the books." It has something quite impersonal about it. Commandment, on the other hand, is that which is addressed to me *personally.* The legislation of the Torah is merely the constitution of the ancient Hebrew commonwealth. Only the Jew who can lift a given "law" from the level of "legislation" to that of a "commandment" addressed to him personally, only he can really re-enact the moment of Revelation, and only he can experience God as the "Giver of the Torah." The constant Jewish task, therefore, is that confrontation of the Torah which waits for God to utter the "Thou shalt!"

Simply to do things because they were written down long ago is hardly a religious exercise. If the meaning of the commandments is that the Jew re-lives his people's experience of God, then he must become personally involved in the commandments. By reflecting on this need to re-live it all and be in a particular relationship with God, the Jew hears God telling him to do this or that.

And what has all this to do with Sinai? The laws and commandments of the Torah do not all go back to that moment—at any rate, not in the form in which we read them today. They have evolved in the course of the centuries. Different circumstances called forth different responses. Life in the days of the Hebrew monarchy was different from life in the days of the Judges. And the generations engaged in the task of settling in Palestine faced different problems from those that beset the wanderers in the desert. Yet all the different responses to all the different challenges were made from the perspective of the initial commitment at Sinai, of the "We shall do and we shall hearken" with which the people obligated themselves in the days of Moses. The "giving of the Torah," therefore, is not confined to the occasion at Sinai. It is, as a modern scholar has pointed out, "a concept and a generalization, limited to no single concretization or instance." But it was natural for the biblical writers to link all the legislation, and all the teaching, which, in any case, grew out of the Covenant at Sinai, with that covenant itself.

What parts of the Torah really and truly took on their present form already at Sinai we shall probably never know—though scholars are still engaged in the discussion of that subject. But for our *religious* orientation, for the *meaning* which Torah can have for us, this hardly matters. However, since our imagination does crave some kind of concrete image, which craving remains unsatisfied by both the poetry of Exodus 19, and the "specially created voice" of the medieval Jewish philosophers, we may well turn to another part of the Bible where the making of a covenant and the acceptance of commandments is described.

To say that this or that is "Torah from Sinai" really means that, in the course of Jewish history, it followed the process begun at Sinai and is therefore a synonym for "God's commandment." Hence even institutions which developed later can be called "Torah from Sinai." Since God has no vocal organs, the reference to the "specially created voice," according to some Jewish thinkers, is that when it is said "God spoke" it means He created a special "voice" for the purpose so that the people could hear.

There is an account of a "covenant," entered into by the people in the days of Ezra, the circumstances of which we find described in chapters 8 through 10 of the Book of Nehemiah. The assembled people listen to Ezra's words of exhortation, they join in religious observances, and, as the culmination, we read: "Because of all this we make a firm covenant and write it, and our princes, our Levites, and our priests set their seal to it." (Nehemiah 10:1.)

Then follows a list of the signatories. And then: "The rest of the people, the priests, the Levites, the gatekeepers, the singers, the temple servants, and all who have separated themselves from the peoples of the lands to the law of God, their wives, their sons, their daughters, all who have knowledge and understanding, join with their brethren, their nobles, and enter into a curse and an oath to walk in God's law which was given by Moses, the servant of God, and to observe and do all the commandments of the Lord and His ordinances and His statutes." (Nehemiah 10:29f.)

After this come individual provisions of the Law. And this is followed by the statement: "We also lay upon ourselves commandments." (Nehemiah 10:33.)

There are no thunders and lightnings here, no mountains trembling, and no earth shaking. There is just an assembly of the whole people proclaiming: "We also lay upon ourselves commandments!" But they did so in response to a soul-stirring religious experience. It was one of those moments in Jewish history when God had revealed Himself to Israel.

The covenant in the days of Ezra was, however, only one of several such covenants which modern scholarship believes to have been found in the biblical record. Each one of the several legal "codes" of the Pentateuch, the existence of which we have mentioned in our first chapter, is said to have been accepted by the people, at various stages of their history, at just such a covenantal assembly. It may not be too farfetched to assume that the pattern of all such covenantal assemblies was set at Sinai, that there are essential features in the covenant described in the Book of Nehemiah which this last of the biblical covenants has in common with the first of these covenants—the covenant at Sinai. Here, too, after a moment of supreme religious awareness, the Children of Israel constituted themselves as God's "chosen people." And, to carry out that task, they "laid upon themselves commandments," they accepted certain obligations in both the "ethical" and the "ritual" realms. And henceforth, all similar commandments and obligations, which, time and again, the people would lay upon themselves, became part and parcel of that Torah which Israel received at Sinai. The continued process of law-making was but a repercussion of that same Love of God which "chose" Israel and initiated the "covenant."

*Note how Petuchowski stresses at one and the same time the
people's part in all this and yet their awareness that they were
meeting their God. Thus revelation is seen as a long process in
Jewish history with special "covenants" made from time to time.
This kind of approach does not fly in the teeth of Biblical
scholarship, which recognizes various strata in the Pentateuch and
in subsequent Biblical literature and yet it safeguards the concept
of God's commandments.*

Admittedly, the description we have attempted above is not the "traditional" one. It is a 20th-century interpretation—and , as such, it differs no less from the interpretation offered by Maimonides in the 12th century than Maimonides himself differed from his talmudic predecessors. Our interpretation differs from traditional notions in this above all: that the scholarly doubts about the Mosaic authorship of the complete Pentateuch have been taken into consideration. The *fact* of Revelation, and of "the giving of the Torah," is here considered quite independently of any one notion—modern or traditional—about the Torah's literary history.

Petuchowski puts the word "traditional" in quotes. While he admits that his interpretation is untraditional in that "the scholarly doubts about the Mosaic authorship of the complete Pentateuch have been taken into consideration," he believes that there is no one, simple way of interpreting the facts—that in Judaism's long history there have been many interpretations. Consequently, a modern interpretation which safeguards the really basic thing, the idea of Revelation, is, in this very important respect, "traditional."

Strange as it may seem, however, the *"Mosaic* authorship of the Pentateuch," though generally assumed by Jews throughout the centuries, was not at all what really mattered to Judaism. What was emphasized was the fact that the Torah come from *God!* Rabbinic literature calls him a heretic who asserts: "The whole Torah was dictated by God, but this particular matter was written by Moses of his own accord." One could, in other words, maintain the "Mosaic authorship," and still be called a "heretic." For what mattered here was not really the human agency through which God gave His Torah, but the fact that it was *God* who gave it. If this was denied, then no belief in the accomplishments of *Moses* could save the concept of Torah. And we have been concerned in this chapter with just this: that behind the literary history of the Pentateuch, behind the various legal codes and narratives, there was the impact of the Love of God, the momentum of a Revelation, which, in a profound sense, enables us to this day to offer our praise unto Him Who is the "Giver of the Torah."

Everybody in the days of the Rabbis believed that Moses wrote the Pentateuch (because, before the rise of modern scholarship there was no reason for them to have believed otherwise), even the non-believer in Revelation who held that Moses wrote it of his own accord. Therefore, the Rabbis do not speak of the "Mosaic Authorship" of the Pentateuch, but say that "the Torah is from Heaven." Nowadays, as Petuchowski has said, we find it hard to believe in the Mosaic authorship of the whole of the Pentateuch, but this does not really matter since the important thing is to believe that the Torah is of divine origin and, if we follow Petuchowski's interpretation, we can still believe this, albeit in a different sense from that of the "tradition." This should be compared with Rosenzweig regarding the "Redactor."

The Commandments create character

How the Torah makes for the improvement of character.

Samson Raphael Hirsch (1808-1888) was the great leader of Orthodox Judaism who successfully presented Orthodox teachings in a form understandable to educated Jews in the modern world. In this passage he describes how the ideal of Torah has implications for the formation of a wholesome character. The Torah is not only a matter of doing the right things but of being the right person. The passage is in Rabbi I. Grunfeld's translation in Judaism Eternal, *Selected Essays from the Writings of Rabbi Samson Raphael Hirsch,* Volume Two *(The Soncino Press, London, 1956, pages 172-179).*

The great inherent quality in the Jewish character is compassion. The Jew who is not compassionate to all that God has created is no true Jew. To him who is merciful to his fellow creatures Heaven will be merciful, but he who shows no mercy to his fellow creatures can count on no mercy from above.

The Talmud tells us that the great Redactor of the Mishna, Rabbi Judah the Prince, said to a calf that fled to him for protection while it was being taken to the slaughterhouse: "Go, for you were created for this!" Thereupon they said above: "Because he showed no mercy let him be condemned to long years of pain and suffering." One day his maid swept up some baby weasels and was going to drown them. "Let them live," he said to her. "His tender mercies are over all His works." Then they said above: "Because he has shown mercy, mercy will be shown to him," and his pains ceased.

These and the following ideas are all taken by Hirsch from sources such as the Talmud and he tries to show how these ancient teachings are of the utmost relevance to the world today. He hardly adds any comments of his own, preferring, on the whole, to let the Rabbis speak for themselves. Note that in the story of Rabbi Judah and the calf it is not suggested that it is wrong to kill animals for food. Nevertheless it is wrong to be so unfeeling as to urge the calf to go to its slaughter willingly, as it were, because it was created for this purpose. The story might also be intended to suggest that animals were created for other purposes besides that of merely being used by humans.

The Talmud teaches that it is a man's duty to manage his possessions wisely, since no man has a right to squander and waste his possessions. At the same time, however, it is his duty to open his hand at all times to help others, to assist human and charitable objects. One who simply burns more oil than is necessary has transgressed the prohibition in Deuteronomy (20,20) not to destroy, the prohibition not to cut down trees for food being extended to the destruction or waste of anything useful.

But the Talmud also teaches that one tenth of one's annual income should be set aside and kept ready for charitable objects, a provision which was so conscientiously carried out in Jewish life that the Rabbis found it advisable to limit the amount given in charity to a fifth of one's property as a maximum, so that the donor himself should not be reduced to seeking assistance. The Rabbis never ceased to emphasize the importance of charity; they gave meticulous instructions about the right and proper manner of bestowing charity, both privately and communally. They uttered dire warnings against any attempt to evade this responsibility. On the other hand they bade people to undergo the greatest privations in order not to require assistance. But to carry this self-denial to the point of endangering one's health and that of one's dependants, they called sinning against oneself. Whoever, on the other hand, accepts charity when he does not need it will, before he dies, find himself really in need of it. All the same, one who needs charity and refuses to accept it will not die before he has himself been able to give charity to the poor.

In the matter of giving a tenth of one's income to charity it might be argued nowadays that this is fulfilled in part at least by paying income tax, some of which is used for the alleviation of suffering. Yet that is hardly an act we do because we wish to practice mercy.

The Talmudic teaching is never tired of urging us to cultivate those characteristics and qualities that make for proper and due fulfilment of our duties to society, and warning us against acquiring those opposite qualities which stand in the way of proper social behaviour. Pride, anger, quarrelsomeness, hastiness, self-opinionatedness, cocksureness, obstinacy, stiff-neckedness, impudence, flattery, lying, suspiciousness, ambition, covetousness, greed, envy, implacability, ingratitude, malice, misery, levity, hatred, unsociability and so forth, these are all vices against which the Talmud is constantly warning us. On the other hand, it praises, in the highest terms, modesty and humility, composure, patience and forbearance, a conciliatory, peaceable and compliant attitude, decency, friendliness and affability, truthfulness and straightforwardness, lenience, moderation and abstemiousness, self-control, generosity, contentment, gratitude, readiness to rejoice with others, cheerfulness, earnestness and sincerity, love, truthfulness and loyalty, calmness, etc.

We bring here a few examples which will give an idea of the moral teachings of the Talmudic sages. Haughtiness is an abomination to God like idolatry, and on a par with the denial of God. God says of the haughty person, we two cannot live together in the world. The man who goes about with his neck haughtily outstretched pushes the presence of God out of the world. When God was about to reveal Himself, He passed over the high mountains and the high trees and chose the lowly Mount Sinai and the thornbush. Thus God avoids the haughty and dwells with the modest.

These sayings, all from the Talmud, explain themselves, but Hirsch has skillfully chosen those relevant to human life even in our day.

The angry man is dominated by a power that should have no place in a man's soul, for it is said, "You shall have no strange gods within you". Do not vex yourself and you will not sin, even as you must not become intoxicated, so that you should not sin. When a man is angry he is exposed to all the evils of hell, he does not respect God Himself, he forgets all that he has learnt and becomes stupid. Anger brings no good. The angry man has nothing but his anger, and his life is no life. God loves the man who does not give way to anger, who does not become intoxicated, who does not insist on his right. Those who suffer affront but do not return the affront, those who hear themselves demeaned and insulted but do not answer with insult, who do everything out of love for God and are joyful with what they must endure, of them it is said: "They that love Him will be as the sun when he goeth forth in his might." Be hard to anger and easy to pacify. He who overlooks injustice committed against him will have the injustice that he commits overlooked. He who forgives is forgiven by God. Remove the wisps of straw from your own garment before you try to remove them from your neighbour's clothes. Cleanse yourself before trying to cleanse your neighbour.

The remark about forgiving injustice does not mean, of course, that no one can have a court case. If everyone is prepared to allow injustice to go unchecked, criminals would have an easy time of it. The meaning is rather that we should not go through life constantly complaining of the wrongs others do to us, even if occasionally we have good cause for complaint.

Contention is like a river bursting its dam. If it is not held in check at once it cannot be restrained. Happy is the man who does not answer back. He escapes a hundred evils. Do you know how to recognise the moral nobility of a man? He is the first who in a conflict keeps silent.

Judge every man from his good side. Judge no man till you have once been in his plight. Be not indifferent to the judgment of your fellow-men. As man should appear clean before God so he should let his actions appear justified before men, and invite no false seeming upon himself.

Have no evil eye that grudges your neighbour's good. Look with a friendly eye upon his prospering, and rejoice in his joy. Envy, covetousness and ambition destroy a man's world. Be not envious. The name that belongs to you, the place you deserve are yours. No man can take away what is destined for another. Be content with what you have. Contentment is wealth. Not everyone can sit at two tables (the material and the spiritual, this world and the next). Don't wish for shoes too big for your feet.

*The teachings here on contentment might appear to decry all
ambition, which may seem to have been Hirsch's intention. But
many of his followers in Germany attained positions of great
prominence in medicine, the arts, science, banking, university
teaching, etc. So that they must have had some ambition. The meaning
is rather that a man should know his strengths and his weaknesses.
He should not be miserable simply because some attainments are
beyond his ability, and he should not seek to further his ambitions
at the expense of the happiness of others.*

The higher a man stands in the esteem of his fellow-men, the more
his actions should be an example to others, the more strictly is he
called upon to keep his ways and actions clean and unspotted, the
more liable is he to fall into this way of sinning, and the more carefully
must he avoid any appearance of wrong-doing; he must not allow
himself things that would be permitted to others. Hence a higher
standard is set for the Jewish people, which has been chosen to carry
God's teaching and man's duty to God through the world than for the
rest of the world, a higher standard for the priests than for the rest of
the people; from the teachers, from all in whom is presumed a famil-
iarity with the Law and consequent knowledge of what is according to
God's will, there is required a higher standard than from the bulk of
the people. The usual remark made about such persons is: "A man
who is respected and looked up to is something different."

*The final sentence is a quote from the Talmud. On occasion the
Talmud asks why did so-and-so do this or that since the Law does
not oblige him to be so strict. The answer is that as a man who is
looked up to he has to preserve far higher standards.*

Particularly is the Jewish people always reminded of its responsibility
in this respect, in its relations with non-Jews. Jews are told to deal
more honestly and fairly with non-Jews. A wrong committed against a
fellow-Jew is an ordinary sin, but a wrong committed against a non-Jew
is in addition the capital sin of profaning the name of God, the sancti-
fication of which is Israel's mission and destiny, and one of the objects
for which Israel was dispersed among the nations.

*This passage has been slightly abbreviated, but it conveys Hirsch's
insistence that the life of the Torah means having a good character so*

that one is able to live in harmony with others and perform a useful function in society. After this passage he goes on to show how, for example, all this applies to man as a member of a family, of a community, and he, therefore, shows how misguided are ignorant attacks on the Talmud for alleged anti-social teachings.

With regard to the ethics of Judaism, we can say that all modern Jewish groups interpret them in about the same way, and give them very heavy emphasis.

Ethics are the essence

The ethical and social content of the Torah.

Hermann Cohen (1842-1918) was teacher of philosophy at Marburg University and one of the foremost thinkers of modern times. He was particularly interested in Judaism as an ethical religion. The following extract on The Nature of Hebrew Prophecy *is from the translation appearing in* Contemporary Jewish Thought, A Reader, Volume IV *of the* Great Books Series *(B'nai B'rith, Washington, D.C., 1963, pages 154-158).*

From the point of view of social awareness, the purest spring of religion is to be found in Hebrew prophecy. . . . By virtue of the fact that the prophets separated the love of God from mysticism and, without following the path of science still endeavored to prepare a way for knowledge within the domain of love, they became the *founders of social religion* and therein of the social conscience as such. How were they able to accomplish this? Had the prophets halted at God, this development of the social conscience would not have been possible. They did not concentrate on God alone, however, but rather set Him into relationship, connection, and interaction with man. Consequently the problem of love arose for them not with God but rather in connection with man. It was man that the prophets aimed to understand—only not on the basis of a science of man. Indeed such an understanding of man, on this basis, was impossible even for Plato; and he sought

assistance in his endeavor from his Idea. In their effort to understand man the prophets sought assistance from their concept of God.

Cohen means that the love man has for his fellows, without which all social life would be impossible, cannot be understood merely by considering human life and society as one would do any other science. Science can only tell us that men do love their fellows at times, but even Plato, the great philosopher, was unable to explain why this is so simply by studying man. Plato, in fact, had to fall back on the Idea. For Plato all things we see on earth have as a counterpart an Idea, which is their source. This was thought of as altogether more pure and refined than anything we can know here on earth. Hence, for Plato, the love men have for one another is ultimately based on the pure Idea of love. Cohen says that the great Hebrew prophets found the source of this love in God. But the importance of the idea of God was, for them, the possibility of human love and benevolence and justice here on earth. This is what Cohen means when he refers rather slightingly to "mysticism." He maintains that the contribution of the prophets did not include concern with the mystical love of God as revealed in social relationships. They did not "halt at God."

It would, of course, be unthinkable that the Hebrew prophets, alone among the seers of mankind should have excogitated the notion of the Unique God without any stimulus from speculation. Only their reflection concerning God as the Unique Being remained without the support of science. This is decisive, since it was responsible for the transfer of the center of gravity from the entire domain of metaphysics to the problem of morality exclusively. Not only were questions concerning God approached in this manner, but also those relating to man and indeed to an even greater degree. Thus it was that for the prophetic mind the God deriving from Babylonia, as the author of heaven and earth, became transformed at the outset into a God of human beings, the Creator of mankind.

The Hebrew prophets were also thinkers. In Cohen's words they "excogitated the notion of the Unique God" by means of speculation. However, theirs was not a "scientific" study of man arrived at by pure thought, but arose from their consideration of what God meant to them. Consequently, they were not philosophers concerned with abstract metaphysics, but profound moralists deeply occupied in discovering the claims of "social religion." In Cohen's words they

*were less concerned with the fact that God created heaven and earth
as with the fact that He created mankind.*

Presently the prophets were to hail even God to judgment before the legal tribunal of human justice. Yet for them man was not ideally the son of God, the demigod, the hero; for them it was rather man in all his weakness who was the paradigm. This weakness was primarily moral, and so it is man's sinfulness that determined the primal image of him. But just as the philosophy of morality remained alien to the prophets, so also did tragedy. Hence they did not stop with either guilt or punishment—the two sides of fate which form the poetic background of all human existence, but rather they tore away the wrappings of dignity that had become attached to this duality of guilt and punishment. They interpreted suffering not as the fate of man, but as a stage in the evolution of the concept of his human condition. By eliminating this basic tragic concept, they did away with the primeval mythical idea of the envy of the gods. In the prophetic interpretation God is the Good Being, not goodness as such. If suffering also derives from Him, it is not an evil, but it must be placed in context in the development of the good, for which the Good God is responsible.

*The prophets thought so highly of man that they taught that God
could be challenged by man to deal justly—"before the legal tribunal
of human justice." Yet for all their high opinion of man they knew of
all his weaknesses. Indeed, this was the whole point—that weak and
immoral man could yet be spurred on to lead a good ethical life. The
Greeks often spoke of guilt and punishment and much of Greek
tragedy is about precisely this. But for Cohen this is to invest man
with too much dignity. He is not as great as all that. The Greek tended
to think of guilt and punishment in terms of man's greatness so that
the gods were jealous of him. No, said the Hebrew prophets,
according to Cohen. This is man, a weak creature prone to injustice.
God is not envious of him but on the contrary wants him to lead a
better life and encourages him to do so. The remark about the "Good
Being, not goodness as such" probably relates to the Greek gods who
were "good" because it was their being gods which made them such
so that man, who was not a god, could never be good. But for the
prophets God is the Good Being and therefore man, too, in his own
small way, could have some approach to God's Being by himself
doing good.*

That henceforth suffering was set apart from guilt and was not identi-fied with punishment is one of the most significant consequences of monotheism, and one of the deepest clarifications of the social prob-lem. For suffering constitutes the most difficult indictment against the goodness of God. Yet if this problem is thought of primarily in con-nection with death, myth remains in sole control of the field. Death is an image of the fate that controls gods and men; of this fate, as far as human beings are concerned, death is a manifestation, and inevi-tably befalls all men. Wherever thought takes this line, nothing remains for human morality to accomplish, and so it remains necessarily estopped at the level of mysticism. If there is to be any evocation of ethical activity against suffering, attention had to be averted from the common human fate of sickness and death. Henceforth the quest would have to be not for the biological causes of human misery but rather for the sociological ones. Accordingly, for the Hebrew prophet, the *pauper* became the symbol of man.

The Greeks believed in fate. Everything is fated to happen as it does. If a man is guilty and is punished for his sins, this too is fated. Even the gods themselves are fated to act as they do. But in a fatalistic view there is nothing for man to do and nothing that he can really do. All is fated from the beginning. In such a view morality would have little meaning and all speculation about it would dissolve into "mysticism." If one dwells on suffering, for example, as the common lot of mankind, there is little motive for research into the alleviation of suffering. But if one declares, as the prophets did, that a good deal of human suffering is unnecessary and should be fought against, then the way is open to a real struggle against evil. The pauper, the poor man who has nothing, becomes the symbol of man. Unlike the symbol of the cripple, for instance, who cannot be cured, the symbol of the "pauper" suggests that human misery can be removed and that it is the duty of the good man to do this.

With this fundamental idea as a guide, we may follow the entire evolu-tion of the prophetic movement. God was not interpreted as the Father of heroes, and such worthies were not represented as being His favorites; rather was it held to be true that God loves the stranger. In polytheism the stranger, apart from the fact that he may be shown hospitality, was regarded as the opposite of the ideal man, who must necessarily be a member of the in-group. Indeed the stranger is represented as a barbarian. But once the God of the group is represented as loving the barbarians, and regards hostile nations as his own quite like his own people of Israel, the horizon of mankind becomes luminous. The Messianic movement advances and accelerates this evolution, which culminates in internationalism.

Because of this particular insight which the prophets had, the ideal for them became the creation of a better society. They were always dwelling on the evils of life which can be removed so as to persuade men to remove them—and this led eventually to the Messianic idea i.e., that one day these social evils and injustices as well as war between nations would be eradicated.

We must now turn to another consequence of the prophetic attitude —the one leading in the direction of socialism. Even as God loves the stranger, so too He is practically always represented as loving the widow and the orphan, for all of them are subject to social oppression, from which the justice of God will liberate them.

Cohen is not using the term "socialism" in a political sense. He means a social conscience which cares for the widow, etc.

Yet no matter how consistently the prophets invoked law and justice, and proclaimed their God to be the God of justice, they did not remain content with this abstraction, which constituted a sort of knowledge. They directed their attention to the heart of man, which they regarded as the only treasure trove of his spirit, and in this manner they evoked sympathy as the form of awareness corresponding to suffering. In the Hebrew language there is an original term for sympathy or pity, one that is derived from the word for womb (rechem). This is the feeling that God feels for the pauper; this is the feeling whereby a man should discover for himself the common human being behind the poor.

The prophets did not simply speak to man's mind. They did not simply offer a philosophy of ethics. They tried to teach men how to have sympathy in their hearts, to feel with the unfortunate as even God was said to do. The most common Hebrew word for compassion is raḥamanut, which, says Cohen, is derived from the Hebrew word meaning "womb." Man's love, sympathy and compassion for the poor, as well as God's, is compared to the feeling a mother has for her baby.

Accordingly, sympathy is not a passion, nor a physiological effect which man has in common with animals. Rather is it a spiritual factor or perhaps one might say, a surrogate of the spirit. In it one may observe how the entire power of a philosophy of life struggles to achieve awareness. Indeed one would have to doubt the justice of God, as well as His goodness and providence, did not such sympathy become one of the powers of the human consciousness, which may overcome the scepticism that emanates from the so-called human mind.

This sympathy and compassion has a "spiritual" quality. It is not found among animals. As a pure philosopher, man might come to be very skeptical, including skepticism about all human goodness. But then this spiritual quality of compassion brings light into his life. He discovers that as a human being he does care for others and is moved to help life's unfortunates.

Of all the human sufferings, poverty alone holds the greatest interest for me, as representing the heaviest fetter of man's burden of pain. Man might even conquer death itself but poverty would remain his indelible mark. It is one of the most fateful deceptions that poverty should have come to be regarded as the retribution for man's guilt. Actually on such a fallacious view, it is impossible to arrive at the truth of God and little at the truth of man, and indeed not even at the first discovery of man. It is sympathy that first makes possible the discernment of the common humanity in mankind. In sympathy the suffering of another becomes one's own, and thereby the other man becomes a fellow-man.

There was a widely held ancient idea that man is poor because the gods will it so and that therefore it is impious to try to remove poverty. This makes of the pauper an outcast. But, says Cohen, whoever has sympathy and compassion puts himself in the place of the poor man and feels with him. The poor man then becomes no outcast but a fellow human being who has to be helped.

It is significant that Plato had not yet developed an idea of man. It is equally significant that this step forward in the doctrine of ideas was achieved by Philo, the Jew. To his mind man needed this distinctive aspect of the value of knowledge, as much as he did the mathematical ideas of nature. Nor was Philo satisfied with just the idea of the good. To be sure, Plato himself had already advanced the idea of God as the Good, but this idea had remained one-sided and incomplete as long as man did not attain a personal share in the Good.

Philo, speaking as a Jew, did not simply affirm that God is Good but that man, as created by God, could share in that Goodness by doing good.

It was the Hebrew prophets who discovered this unique human value, and this discovery derived from their social consciousness. *They equated the poor with the righteous.* This equation of the categories is the decisive climax in the evolution of Messianism. As a consequence of this development the Messiah himself became the standard-bearer of poverty. He takes upon himself all the guilt of mankind because he has shouldered all the suffering, quite without the charm of heroic strength or superhuman beauty. He eschews all participation in the aesthetic attractions of the world, and in his social misery he represents only the collective misery of mankind.

The Rabbis speak of the Messiah as "poor" and "miserable." He is not a brave Greek hero, refusing to bow to fate. This means that the Messiah cannot come and the world cannot be redeemed unless men know all the miseries of human existence and learn to fight against them. Poverty is not an heroic thing but something one must fight against. Far from the poor being outcasts, they are the righteous ones, because this is part of mankind's common misery which righteousness demands should be removed.

It was in this wise that the Faust poem of the ancient Bible, the Book of Job, enters into the sphere of messianism. Once the prophets had expounded to the people the view that a man does not sin or suffer because of his ancestors, people were bound to ask what then was the source of evil in man? Instead of raising this metaphysical question, the prophets felt that it was necessary for the people to learn to ask what is the source of suffering among men, and that means, what is the significance of poverty. First it was necessary for men to realize the fallacy of attributing this to some guilt in the sufferer; and on the positive side they had to develop the insight that the poor man had to be regarded as the thoroughly good man. This insight was not to be shaken by any concept of God or of man, or by an experience of the world. God is the God of righteousness, and He would help the man beset by poverty. He is the God of world history, and He would make good for humanity what the individual has to suffer. As the God of goodness He can impose the suffering of poverty upon man only out of the light of goodness.

The book of Job deals with the problem of suffering but it does not suggest that an explanation is forthcoming which makes so much sense of suffering that it is no longer seen as an evil. The prophets and Biblical writers generally were not concerned, according to Cohen, with working out a defense of God, but with trying to show what God wants man to do in fighting evil.

Finally, the knowledge of His goodness brings me to the insight that the poor man is the pious and God-fearing one, and indeed the favorite of God. Obviously this conclusion does not result from any science; and hence it is not an idea of the Good either. Nor is it an idea of some abstract good that may be applied to things. Rather is it something that becomes concrete and personal in man. And it is in regard to man that there is first enkindled love for God. . . .

Finally Cohen says that, far from considering the poor as an outcast, prophetic teaching thought of him as being particularly worthy because he knows at first hand the terrible nature of suffering. So he is a kind of living witness to the truth that compassion matters. This statement of Cohen should be compared with the articles on suffering mentioned earlier in this book.

Israel

I S JUDAISM a *religion* with the Jewish people its exponents, or should the idea of Jewish peoplehood be stressed so as to yield the thought that the Jews are really a *nation?* This has been the central problem surrounding the whole concept of the people Israel in modern times. Here, too, three attitudes have emerged.

The extreme Reform position in the last century was that the Jews are simply citizens of the country of their birth, or the one which gave them a home, and that is all. The only difference between the German Jew, for instance, and the German non-Jew is in matters of religion. Both are German but the Jew, in a well used phrase, is a "German of the Mosaic persuasion." The eventual return to Zion has no place at all in this theory. Even the use of the Hebrew language in prayer is not held to be essential because language is a national not a religious matter.

At the exact opposite extreme is the attitude of secular nationalism. According to this view the Jews are primarily a nation like other nations. Religion, in this view, is a matter for the individual. There are religious Jews and there are non-religious Jews, and what unites them is belonging to the same *people*. They are members of the Jewish nation. This view was unrealistic before the rise of Zionism but then it became a matter of practical politics quite capable of realization.

The third attitude has some of each idea but, particularly because they are combined, they now come out differently. This position says the Jews are a religious people and Judaism is a folk faith. Moses Hess, perhaps the earliest modern Zionist thinker, stresses the national idea and accuses those Jews who fail to accept it of moral cowardice. They lack, he suggests, the courage to declare openly that they are different from their neighbors. Herzl is the great practical dreamer in whose thought, and more especially in whose work, the national idea receives its most powerful expression. With the establishment of the State of Israel many of the old problems no longer have much meaning but, of course, many new ones loom large. The declaration made at the establishment of the State of Israel reflects the nationalist view but could not avoid a reference to God.

Almost all modern Jewish thinkers have found the creation of the State of Israel and its development a source of great moral and religious pride. These views are so widespread that they are assumed as the positive background to the remainder of the discussion. For ever since the beginning of Zionism a series of critical questions have been asked which, since the creation of the State of Israel, have taken new form.

Rabbi Chen points out an unusual but highly significant difficulty. Just as there is tension between Jewish particularism and universalism, there is tension between the claims of the individual and those of his group. Rabbi Chen believes that an overstressing of the national idea might result in a diminution of the individual Jew.

Nachman Krochmal, the earliest thinker represented here, is one of the very few modern Jews to try to create a philosophy of Jewish history. He is thoroughly modern for his day, beginning with a theory of nationalism yet insisting that this must be spiritual for Jews to be true to their genius.

Ahad Ha-Am makes his spiritual Zionism far more secular. On this view the State of Israel, when established, will serve as a spiritual center for Judaism. It should be noted carefully that Ahad Ha-Am does not use the term "spiritual" in a religious sense but as referring to intellectual, cultural and moral values.

For Morris Joseph the spiritual aspect of Jewishness requires an anti-nationalistic view. He claims that Jewish nationalism is a hindrance to the universalistic teachings of Judaism. Joseph represents the "mission of Israel" view in which Jewish dispersion among the nations is part of God's providential care for mankind and His plan for its ennoblement. That view has almost entirely disappeared from modern serious discussion. Far more characteristic of the present critical stance is the one taken by Rabbi Maybaum. He accepts the Zionist idea but with important reservations, as his sermon printed here on the Jewish national anthem shows.

The older anti-Zionism was connected with a positive doctrine about the coming of a Messianic Age for all man, as the excerpt from Morris Joseph shows so well. That nineteenth century optimism has itself come under the most serious sort of criticism. Thus, Steven Schwarzschild puts forward the highly original view that our times demand a return to the doctrine of a personal Messiah. Since this is also connected with the idea of after-life and Judaism has something to say on this question as well as on the concerns of this life, it seemed appropriate to conclude with a passage on this doctrine.

Free Jews and a Jewish State

How Western Jews should treat Jewish nationalism.

Theodor Herzl (1860-1904) is the man more than any other responsible for the emergence of the State of Israel, which came into being fifty years after he had worked for it. At first Herzl's idea was of a Jewish State anywhere in the world, but eventually he saw that this dream could only be realized in the ancient land of Palestine, the home of the Jewish people. The following extracts are from The Diaries of Theodor Herzl (edited and translated with an Introduction by Marvin Lowenthal, The Dial Press, Inc., 1956, pages 79-82) and describe his first visit to London to elicit support for his ideas. Palestine had not at that time been chosen for the site of the proposed National Home.

November 23, (1895).

In the evening with the Chief Rabbi at the other house, in the City. He has two houses. The one in the City he occupies from Friday till Sunday. Accordingly I drove to Finsbury Square. I kept knocking at the door for some while. Behind it I heard subdued whispers. At last the door opened, disclosing a dimly lit hall, and I made out a surprising picture: a bevy of young girls who had waited in silence, as though afraid, and who now withdrew into the shadows. I took them to be one of the rabbi's Sabbath-school classes. He told me afterwards that his daughter was giving an amateur-entertainment-concert-recitation-young girls' tea-party.

Later on, Mr. Joseph, Adler's brother-in-law, came to dinner to meet me. Everything English, with old Jewish customs breaking through. It drove home to me the feeling that Jewish ways need not be ridiculous, as they are among us in Austria where the heart has gone out of our observances.

And so, after we ate I put on my top hat, like the others, and listened to the rabbi recite the after-dinner blessing.

Of course I had told the Chief Rabbi, as I had told Zadok Kahn and Güdemann, that I was not thereby responding to a religious impulse. But assuredly I would pay no less respect to the faith of my fathers than to other faiths.

After the meal we men sat by ourselves, and somewhat later we were joined by Elkan Adler, a lawyer and the Chief Rabbi's brother.

I expounded my subject.

The Chief Rabbi remarked: "That is the idea of *Daniel Deronda*." I said: "I do not claim the idea is new. It is two thousand years old. The only novelty lies in the method whereby I launch the idea and then organize the Society, and finally the State. That is to say, not I myself, for I shall withdraw from the execution of the project, which must be an impersonal operation. I am merely creating the organ which will have to direct the thing."

Mr. Joseph—a nice, thoroughly anglicized, slow-thinking and long-winded old man, by profession an architect — advanced the familiar objections: the Jews were not suitable human material; the experience of the Anglo-Russian emigration committees had been distressing; the people were unwilling to work, etc. This, I explained, was due to the faultiness of the experiments. The experiments were bad, the material is good. All the mischief can be laid to the stupid reliance on charity. Charity must cease, and then the *schnorrers* (professional beggars) would disappear. The existent Jewish relief committees must fall in line with us, or they will have to be dissolved.

The Chief Rabbi said: "We shall submit your plan to the Russo-Jewish Committee, and they will decide whether they will participate in your project."

I replied: "Of course the Committee will study the proposal, but I am not submitting it to their disposition. I do not yield to majorities. Whoever goes along with me is welcome. I am turning first to notable Jews who have distinguished themselves by their past efforts, but I do not need them. Naturally, I am bound to be gratified if prominent men march with me. But I am not dependent on them." Elkan Adler has visited Palestine, and he would like us to choose that country. Over there we would have an enormous hinterland.

During all this talk we drank a light claret produced in a Zion colony.

The Jews of England were noted for the way they cared for their fellow-Jews who fled from Russia in the wake of Czarist persecution. As this extract reveals they were more interested in the idea of a Jewish State as a means of helping these unfortunate Jews than as an ideal for for themselves. The Chief Rabbi is Hermann Adler (1839-1911). Eventually he disassociated himself from Herzl's Zionism and called it "an egregious blunder." Notice how Herzl describes the young ladies and their entertainment. He seems to be surprised at the "Western" character of Adler's life, which was very English and at the same time strictly in accordance with Jewish tradition. This impressed Herzl. Herzl was not himself an observant Jew but, as he says here, he had great respect for the faith of his fathers.

Daniel Deronda is the title of a novel by the famous English novelist George Eliot in which ideas similar to those of Herzl are mentioned. Herzl wished first to found a Society for the propagation of his ideas and he believed that this would eventually result in the emergence of the Jewish State. Note how Herzl refuses to look upon Zionism as "charity."

Wine was produced at the time in a "Zion colony." Jews had begun to colonize Palestine but Herzl wished to found a political movement for the establishment of a Jewish State.

November 24, (1895).

Lunched at the home of Sir Samuel Montagu, M.P. A house of English elegance, in grand style. Sir Samuel a splendid old fellow, the best Jew I have met so far. At table he presides over his family—which for the rest is unamiable or perhaps merely well-bred—with the air of a good-natured patriarch. Kosher food, served by three liveried footmen. After lunch, in the smoking room, I expounded my case. I gradually roused him. He confessed to me—in confidence—that he felt himself to be more an Israelite than an Englishman. He would be willing to settle with his entire family in Palestine. He has in mind not the old but a larger Palestine. He will hear nothing of Argentina. He is ready to join our Committee as soon as one of the Great Powers takes the matter seriously. I am to send him my pamphlet before its final publication.

Sir Samuel Montagu (1832-1900) later became the first Lord
Swaythling. At the time when Herzl met him he was an M.P., a
Member of Parliament. Note again how impressed Herzl is with the
combination of gracious Western living and strict Jewish
observance. One of the places mentioned for a possible Jewish
State was Argentina, but Montagu would not hear of this because
he felt that the Jewish heart would only be satisfied with Palestine.
Herzl appears to have been particularly impressed with Montagu—
"the best Jew I have met so far"—because he was interested in the
proposed scheme for himself and his family and not only for the sake
of the poor Jews who had no home.

In the evening, with the "Maccabeans."
Poor dinner, but good reception.
Everyone welcomes me cordially.

**The club members are mostly educated Jews. A smart officer, Captain
(Matthew) Nathan, who was to have gone to Vienna as a military
attaché, but who was unacceptable because of his Judaism.**

**After the meal, Zangwill calls on me—with a somewhat satirical intro-
duction.**

**I speak extemporaneously, dividing my talk into three parts. The first
two in German. Meanwhile, the Reverend Singer takes notes, and after
each part gives an English summary of what I had said.**

The third part I deliver in French.

**My speech is applauded. They confer together in undertones, and
unanimously elect me as an honorary member.**

Then follow the objections, which I refute.

The most important of them: English patriotism.

The "Maccabeans" was a society of English intellectuals,
professional men and artists. Zangwill is the English-Jewish novelist
Israel Zangwill (1864-1926) author of Children of the Ghetto. *The*
Reverend Simeon Singer (1884-1906) was the Rabbi of the New
West End Synagogue in London and author of the Singer Prayer
Book, still widely used in synagogues. Note how Herzl accepts as
the most important objection to his presentation: English
patriotism. This question of whether a Jew can have "dual
loyalties"—to his own country and to the Jewish State—was to come
up again and again in the history of Zionism.

We are not a church

On the question of the Jews as a nation.

Moses Hess (1812-1875) was the first writer to give voice to the new ideas regarding Jewish nationalism which began to find their expression in the middle of the last century. Rome and Jerusalem (translated by Rabbi Maurice J. Bloom, Philosophical Library, New York, 1958), published in 1862, is his statement of his position. Here, some decades before Herzl and for quite idealistic, not merely political reasons, he calls for a Jewish State. His vision may have been more uplifting than Herzl's, but the latter founded an organization and made his ideas a reality. The following is taken from the "Fourth Letter" of Hess' book (pages 25-30).

Like every competent individual, every competent nation has its speciality. To be sure, every man, every member of the historical nations is a political, or as we say today, a social animal; nevertheless, within the social world itself, each one has by nature a special aptitude. The German stresses his "pure human nature." Thus he has no clear conception of his racial prejudices. He does not conceive his racial pride or his spiritual aspirations as pure Germanic expressions, but rather as humanitarian tendencies; without knowing it he honors the latter in theory and the former in practice.

Hess is aware that a powerful argument against Jewish nationalism is that it is better to think in terms of mankind as a whole, in terms of that which all men have in common, rather than in terms of special national concerns. But Hess does not believe that those who put forward this kind of argument are really consistent. They may talk bravely about humanitarian values but in practice they are as narrowly nationalistic as anyone. The Germans, for example, do talk of "pure human nature" but, without realizing it, they are really speaking of "pure German nature." It is true, says Hess, that man has social needs, but he also has the need to express himself as an individual and, by the same token, each nation has its own "specialty." The expression that man is a political animal is Aristotle's but Hess remarks that in his day the word "social" is more frequently used to express the same idea. Even a person who is not a "politician" still has social interests. Hess leads up to his next paragraph in which he accuses the German Jews, who are suspicious of Jewish nationalism, of being really afraid of German Jew-haters whom they wish to appease by pretending that they, the Jews, are as much German as the others. Hess uses the word "race," a term which is very suspect today. There is no such thing as a "pure" race and we have all seen what harm has been done by racist theories in our world. But Hess does not intend the term to be used so much in this way but rather in terms of what we today call "peoplehood."

The cultured German Jews too, have their good grounds for "reluctantly" turning away from Jewish nationalist hopes. Because of the Jew-hatred which surrounds him, the German Jew is only too eager to cast aside everything Jewish and to deny his race. No reform of the Jewish religion is radical enough for the cultured German Jew. Even baptism itself does not save him from the nightmare of German Jew-hatred. I myself have experienced it not only with my opponents but also with my comrades. In every personal fight, they made use of the weapon of HEP which in Germany seldom fails in its effect. The Germans hate the religion of the Jews less than their race. Neither 'radical' reform, (properly so called because it hacks away at the root of Judaism), nor baptism, neither education nor emancipation completely unlocks for the German Jew the portals of social life. They, therefore, seek to deny their origin. The best they can achieve is to "modernize" their first names.

Note the two words Hess puts in quotes—"reluctantly" and "modernize." The German Jews pretend that they are reluctant to give up ideas of Jewish nationalism because of their wider vision

but, in fact, they are only too glad to do so in order to curry
favor with their German neighbors. When they change their names
they claim that they do so in order to be "modern" but what they
really mean is that they prefer not a modern name for an ancient
one but a German name for a Jewish one. "Radical" means
reaching to the roots. Hess remarks that when they speak of radical
reform of the Jewish religion they declare, without knowing it,
that their intention is to strike at the roots of their Jewish faith in
order to be as much like the Germans as they possibly can. No
one quite knows the meaning of HEP but it was a cry used in riots
against Jews in Germany in 1819 and became an anti-Semitic rallying
cry. Some derive the word from the German Hebräer meaning
Hebrews.

The Talmud points out that the Jews in Egypt did not change their
names and their language for that of their environment. Thus they
proved themselves worthier of redemption than later generations when
this practice was frequent. Even our greatest Prophet and Law Giver is
censured because he posed to Jethro as an Egyptian and not as a
Hebrew. For this reason his request to be buried in the Holy Land was
not fulfilled, whereas the bones of Joseph who had never denied his
Hebraic origin, were taken along to the Holy land for burial.

The Scriptural references are to: Exodus 2:13; Deuteronomy
34:4-6; Genesis 50:25. Hess himself changed his name from the
German Moritz to Moses!

The Jewish race is a primary race which, despite climatic influences,
accommodates itself to all conditions and retains its integrity. The
Jewish type has always remained indelibly the same throughout the
centuries. F. A. Strauss, in his "Sinai and Gelgatha," reports: "On the
western slope of Thebes in Egypt, which contains the City of the
Dead, there is the tomb of an architect of the King's buildings. On it
are depicted the different buildings constructed under his direction.
The tomb, according to inscriptions, was finished about the time of
Moses and among the Asiatic slaves the Jewish type is discernible."
Later Egyptian monuments also show us Jews whose resemblance to
our present co-religionist is striking.

The Jewish people, already in antiquity a prey to enemy attack would,
during its dispersion among nations, long ago have been submerged in

the great sea of Indo-Germanic peoples, if it had not continually repro-
duced its type completely. If Judaism owes its immortality to the
splendor of its religious genius, so the latter is indebted to the fruit-
fulness and indestructibility of the Jewish people. What the Bible said
of Jews in Egyptian Bondage is also true of them during the Third Exile:
"But the more they afflicted them, the more they multiplied and the
more they spread abroad . . . And the land was filled with them."

Just as the native land of the Jews, Palestine, grows southern and
northern products so does the people seem to thrive under all climates.

*Hess, in his passage, comes perilously close to racist theories
which are today repudiated by most students of the subject on
scientific grounds.*

Just as it is hardly possible for me to harbor any prejudice against
my own race, which has played the greatest role in world history and
is destined to play an even greater one in the future, so also can I
scarcely condone the prejudice against the Holy Language of Our
Fathers. Its consequence is that Hebrew would be completely eliminated from Jewish life and even ousted from the cemetery by German
inscriptions. I have always been edified by the Hebrew prayers. In my
ears ring the echo of a thousand generations, daily sending forth these
prayers heavenward out of an oppressed heart. These soul-stirring
prayers seldom fail to inspire those who understand them.

The most inspiring thing about the Jewish prayers is that they are
really collective prayers for the whole Jewish community. The pious
Jew is before all else a Jewish patriot. The 'new-fangled' Jew who
denies Jewish nationalism is not only an apostate, a renegade in the
religious sense, but a traitor to his people and to his family. Should it
prove true that the emancipation of the Jews is incompatible with
Jewish nationalism, then the Jew must sacrifice emancipation. But for
anyone who has ever enjoyed a Jewish education, no proof is needed
that the Jew must be, above all, a Jewish patriot. Jewish patriotism is
a natural feeling; it does not need to be demonstrated nor can it
be confuted.

*Hess is pretty violent in his language here. Many have disagreed
with his vehemence and even with his whole concept of "Jewish
patriotism," arguing that the distinctive virtue of Judaism is its
universalism. Of course what Hess means is Jewish self-respect
and love of the Jewish people.*

My grandfather once showed me some olives and dates. "These fruits grow in Eretz Israel!" he informed me with delight. Everything reminiscent of Palestine is regarded by the pious Jew with love and adoration, as ancient mementos of his ancestral home. It is a well known custom that every Jew who dies in Diaspora is given a bit of earth from Palestine for his grave. For otherwise, the dead would have to roll, as it were, under the earth to the Holy Land to merit rest and future resurrection. This custom is based on more than a religious precept. It is more like the use of a citron and palm branch on the Festival of Tabernacles. All the Jews' feasts and fasts, their reverence for traditions which amounts to an apotheosis of everything Hebraic, the whole Jewish religion, and its complete dominance of the domestic life of the Jews, all these have their origin in the patriotism of the Jewish people. The Jewish religion is primarily Jewish patriotism. This, the Jewish "Reformers" who "emancipated" themselves from the Jewish nation, knew quite well. They are very wary of expressing their true sentiments frankly. Even in patriotism, which is a natural and simple sentiment, they seek a double meaning: an ideal (love for Judaism), and a reality (love for the adopted nation), advocating the one or the other according to circumstances.

The early Reformers in Germany omitted from the prayers all references to Zion and Jerusalem as places to which the Jew would one day return. They argued that the place of the Jew is in the land which has offered him hospitality—Germany or France or England—and that his love for Judaism is to be expressed in purely religious, not "patriotic" terms. He should be a German or French or English patriot with a love for Judaism, just as other German or French or English patriots have a love for Christianity. Hess takes issue with this in the most vehement terms. But many would question the correctness of his statement that "The Jewish religion is primarily Jewish patriotism."

Only recently did the belief arise that it was possible to deny Jewish nationalism without endangering the continuation of Judaism. Spinoza still conceived of Judaism as a nationality and believed that the restoration of the Jewish State depended merely on the courage of the Jewish people. Even the otherwise rationalistic Mendelssohn did not know of cosmopolitan Judaism.

I never recall without deep emotion the scenes which I witnessed in my childhood in the house of my pious grandfather at Bonn when the anniversary of the destruction of the Temple drew near. In the first nine days of the month of Ab, the period of mourning, which began three weeks before the fateful ninth day of this month, assumed a really sorrowful character. Even the Sabbath, which occurs during these days of the deepest national sorrow, loses its cheerful festal garb and is very significantly named the "Black Sabbath."

My grandfather was one of those revered scholars who after finishing the daily work of the year round, studied the Talmud until after midnight. Only during the "Nine Days" was this study interrupted. He would then read to his little grandchildren, who had to remain awake till midnight, the tales of the exiles from Jerusalem. The snow white beard of the old man was wet with tears during these readings; nor could we children keep from weeping and sobbing. I recall particularly one passage which never failed to affect both grandfather and grandson:

"When the children of Israel were led into Babylon, bound with chains by the soldiers of Nebuchadnezzar, their way led past the grave of Mother Rachel. As they approached this tomb, 'lamentation and bitter weeping' was heard. It was the voice of Rachel who arose from her grave and bemoaned the fate of her unhappy children."

Ah, indeed, the whole of Jewish life and love revolved about the child. For, in a Jewish heart, love is too abundant to be restricted to one generation; indeed it overflows into future generations. It is because Jewish love looks so far into the future that there were so many divine seers among the Jews. Childlessness is nowhere as sorrowful a state as among the Jews. According to our Rabbis, a childless person is to be mourned like one dead.

Actually Hess' last remarks are a misquotation. The Rabbis do not say that the childless person is to be mourned like one dead but that he is like one dead i.e. there is no one to take his place when he has departed this earth. The whole passage is quite sentimental.

Here again you see plainly the source of the Jewish belief in immortality; it stems from our family love. Our belief in immortality reaches into the past as far as the Patriarchs, and into the future as far as the Messianic Age. The living faith in the continuity of the spirit in history originated from the Jewish family.

This flower of Judaism whose root is Jewish family love and whose stem is Jewish patriotism, this fairest blossom of our national historic religion, has shriveled up into a belief in an atomistic immortality of the individual soul. Through the separation of Christianity from Judaism arose the modern dualism of matter and spirit, killing all unity of life. But when this dualism arrived at its classical expression in the last Christian philosopher, Descartes, the belief in the Eternal in nature and history came forward once again in its original strength from Judaism and stands out today as a bulwark against this spiritual egoism and material individualism.

Hess says that belief in the immortality of the individual soul after the death of the body rather than belief in the immortality of the people is a particularly Christian belief, and an inferior one at that. Instead of dreaming great visions of a whole people, the whole of mankind as immortal, the doctrine of the immortality of the soul calls attention to the narrow life of the individual. It is a selfish belief. Moreover it tends to separate life into two distinct compartments—the material and the spiritual, body and soul. Descartes began by questioning everything. How do we know that anything is true? But he found himself thinking even while engaging in doubting. Consequently he argued that his thinking must be true. A man cannot think whether he can think without at that moment engaging in thought! Consequently, Descartes' famous aphorism is cogito ergo sum: *"I think therefore I am." From this premise he built his entire philosophical system. But since Descartes starts from the mind his system becomes dualistic, it tends to separate mind from body, spiritual from material. Spinoza (the Jew) admits in his system no such dualism and Hess considers this a more noble view of life and sees here the influence of Judaism on Spinoza. But Hess is far too sweeping in his judgment on the immortality of the soul. After all many great Rabbis believed in the immortality of the soul.*

As Christian dualism was exploded by Spinoza in theory, so the continued existence of the ancient Jewish people in the midst of the modern world constituted, through its healthy family life, a practical protest against this disease of dualism. Even today the wholesome influence of the Jewish family life is notable in literature, art and science. How much more will this be so when we will have our own national history and native literature—when the Torah will again go forth from Zion

and the word of the Lord from Jerusalem! This is the single prophecy which is reiterated by many prophets and permeates our whole historic religion.

So, Hess argues, if the Jewish family has been able to produce so many great men on foreign soil, how great a contribution to human destiny will the Jews make when they are permitted to create their own culture on their own soil for their own society.

A home for our culture

What is meant by a spiritual center for Jews.

Ahad Ha-Am was the pen-name of Asher Ginzberg (1856-1927) the
essayist, thinker and Zionist philosopher who developed the idea
of Palestine as a spiritual center for Jews everywhere. He opposed
Herzl as having too political and uncultural view of Zionism. For him
resettling the land had to mean reviving Jewish culture. The
following is from Ahad Ha-Am: Essays, Letters, Memoirs
(translated by Leon Simon, East and West Library, London, 1946,
pages 96-100).

Today the conscience of the world is stirred by the bitter cry of the
homeless and starving Jewish masses. Help is offered from every side,
more or less generously, and in course of time the wanderers will find,
somewhere or other, at any rate a temporary haven of rest. The Jewish
people will not be utterly wiped out. But there is an internal process
of decay which is going on at the same time, silent and unnoticed.
The Jewish people is losing its soul; its great heritage of culture is
crumbling away; and not a voice is raised. How low we have sunk if we
have neither understanding nor feeling for anything except the physi-
cal suffering which cuts us to the quick!

This is a version, which Ahad Ha-Am wrote in Hebrew, of an
address he gave to a conference of Russian Zionists at Minsk in the
summer of 1902. For him political Zionism was not enough and he

*wished to encourage the growth of a specific Jewish culture.
For Ahad Ha-Am, this was not necessarily religious in nature. He
believed that just as the English people, for example, are producing
art, literature and philosophy in the present as in the past, the
Jewish people, in its rebirth, thanks to political Zionism, should
produce great works of Jewish culture. He states in this passage
that the material suffering of the Jews, which is terrible, will
nonetheless be alleviated by generous people with kind hearts—
but surely Jews have dreamed of something more than mere
physical survival.*

True, there are a few Zionists who realise that the spiritual sickness
of which I have spoken threatens our whole future no less than the
dangers to which we are exposed on the material side; and they rightly
draw the conclusion that a home of refuge for the Jewish soul is no
less imperatively necessary than a home of refuge for the homeless
masses of Jews. They imagine, however, that the material and the
spiritual problems are capable of solution by one and the same
method. A healthy and properly ordered Jewish settlement in Palestine, they believe, will automatically provide the necessary basis for a
national rebirth in the spiritual sense; without such a material basis
there can be no security or stability for that spiritual centre of our
nation which we aspire to create.

*The Zionists with whom Ahad Ha-Am here disagrees held that it
was indeed important for Palestine to become the home of the
reborn Jewish spirit. This requires no effort, but will result naturally
from the new situation of security in which the Jews will find
themselves. To talk of a spiritual center without material security is
nonsense and to talk of it where there is material security is
superfluous because it will follow in any event. Ahad Ha-Am
cannot agree with such a facile approach. Zionism must do
something about it if it is serious about Palestine as a spiritual center.*

Now the material settlement admittedly has a bearing on our spiritual
problem, and is indeed necessary to its full solution. I would go further,
and say that in my opinion the whole point of the material settlement
—whether its architects realise it or not—is to provide the foundation
for that spiritual centre of our nation which is destined to arise in
Palestine in response to the insistent urge of the national instinct;

whereas our material problem will not be solved by the acquisition of a home of refuge, because in the great centres of Jewish population the natural increase will always offset the loss due to transfers to the Jewish home, so that in the ordinary course of nature our numbers cannot be reduced by emigration. But it does not by any means follow that we ought not to do anything here and now for the spiritual rebirth. We cannot wait for it to come about automatically when the material settlement in Palestine is sufficiently far advanced. We must admit that that would mean waiting a very long time. A score or a hundred agricultural settlements, however well established, will not of themselves save the Jewish soul, in the sense of bringing about a re-union of our scattered spiritual forces and their concentration in the service of our national culture. For that we shall need a national centre in the fullest sense, with all the manifold and expanding interests, demands and activities that that term connotes. Can we sit and wait for the realisation of this great vision—which nobody expects to come very quickly— and meanwhile allow the process of spiritual decay to go on unchecked?

I maintain, then, that Zionism cannot confine itself to the material work of rebuilding Palestine. We must advance along both lines at the same time. While making every effort to create a large Jewish settlement on sound lines, we dare not neglect to do what is neces- sary to make Palestine a permanent and freely developing centre of our national culture, of our science and scholarship, our art and litera- ture. While gradually assembling the skilled labour that is needed to repair the ruins of our country and restore its past glories, we must also assemble the forces of heart and mind and brain that will repair our spiritual ruins and restore the Jewish people to its rightful place of honour in the comity of human culture. The establishment of a single great school of learning or art in Palestine, or of a single Academy of language and literature, would in my opinion be a national achieve- ment of first-rate importance, and would contribute more to the attainment of our aims than a hundred agricultural settlements. These agricultural settlements are merely so much building material for our future home; they cannot of themselves provide the driving power for a revolution in Jewish life. But a great cultural institution in Palestine, attracting to itself a large number of gifted Jewish scholars, for whom it would provide the possibility of carrying on their work in a Jewish atmosphere, free from repressions and not unduly subject to extraneous influences—such an institution could even now become a source of new inspiration to the Jewish people as a whole and bring about a true revival of Judaism and Jewish culture.

Note how Ahad Ha-Am identifies the spiritual ideals of which he speaks with the kind of topics taught at universities and colleges of art and science. Note also his reference to Jewish scholars being able to carry on their work "free from repressions." In Ahad Ha-Am's day many Jewish scholars were a little afraid of publishing any scholarly work which did not show Jews always in the best light because they were disturbed by what their Gentile neighbors might say. But learning cannot flourish in such an atmosphere. Ahad Ha-Am states here that in a truly Jewish atmosphere there will no longer be a need for Jews to always be concerned with what non-Jews are saying, and they will be able to foster Jewish learning and tell the truth "without repressions." The dream of Ahad Ha-Am was realized by institutions such as the Hebrew University, the founding of which he himself was privileged to witness. He thinks of the influence of such institutions not alone on Palestinian Jewry but on world Jewry. Some of Ahad Ha-Am's critics have been somewhat skeptical of his whole conception of a spiritual center. A university, for example, is no doubt required, but the subjects taught there and the methods of teaching are no different from those obtaining in any other university. There is no special Jewish mathematics or physics, for example, and even Jewish studies are the norm in many universities outside Israel.

I am well aware that this is reversing the usual order of things. The normal and natural development of a nation's life proceeds from the lower to the higher stages. A nation's first care is to make its economic and political position secure; only when that has been satisfactorily accomplished does it turn its mind to less material concerns and produce whatever it is capable of producing in the domain of the spirit. But we Jews are not a new-born nation, just beginning to climb the ladder of progress rung by rung. We climbed the lower rungs of the ladder thousands of years ago, and had reached a high level of culture when our natural progress was forcibly arrested. The ground was cut away from under our feet, and we were left hanging in mid-air, carrying a heavy and valuable load of accumulated culture, but without any sort of basis for healthy life or free development. So things went on for centuries. The Jewish people remained miserably poised between heaven and earth, struggling with all its might to preserve its cultural inheritance and not to fall below the level it had reached in its more prosperous days. And now, when we have some hope of coming down to earth again and building our life on solid natural foundations, are we to be told that we ought to jettison our burden of culture, so as to be better able to concentrate on the material tasks which normally take precedence, and afterwards start again, in the customary fashion, from the bottom of the ladder?

Ahad Ha-Am argues that while, of course, no adequate spiritual life can be built up if there is no physical security, yet, in fact, the Jews did manage somehow to produce a spiritual life even without any security at all. True this was an unhealthy state of affairs but at least it gives the Jew today hope that he need not, and should not, wait fully to establish his material existence before he proceeds to take care of his spiritual existence.

"There is nothing in the universal that is not in the particular." There is no nation so rich as ours in men who combine a highly developed intellect with an elementary ignorance of the alphabet of culture, and are forced to repair this deficiency when they are grown men with well-stocked minds. Solomon Maimon, for example, went to school to learn German and other elementary subjects after he had reached manhood and had won a reputation in Germany as a profound philosopher; and there have been many Jews like him in the last hundred years. What would they have said if somebody had been stupid enough to advise them to forget all they had learnt, and to concentrate all their attention on the primary subjects until they again became educated men by the normal process of advancing gradually from the simpler to the more difficult disciplines?

The Jewish people is in an analogous position, child and grown man in one. Intellectually we emerged from childhood three thousand years ago, and we need an adult's diet; but the circumstances in which we are placed compel us to go to nursery school again and master the alphabet of national life. What are we to do? The answer is that we must start from both ends at once—that is to say, build from the bottom and from the top at the same time. Of course this is not the normal method of nation-building. But then our life is altogether abnormal, and however we may build, the structure will be something without precedent. So it is of no use to look to other nations for guidance. We must do what our peculiar circumstances compel us to do, relying on the strength of will and the patience which have miraculously kept us alive till now and will see us through in the future.

Of course the natural and normal thing for someone who wishes to be educated is to learn the simple things first and then go on to the more difficult. But this only applies if one starts to learn while a child. If a grown-up, who knows a lot but has missed the elementary things, wishes to catch up with these, it would be stupid for him to forget all he knows and start entirely afresh. There were many Jews in such a position because their minds were nourished on the riches of Jewish thought but were unable to acquire even the rudiments of modern culture because they had no access to any kind of schooling. And what is true of individual Jews is true of the nation as a whole since "There is nothing in the universal that is not in the particular." This saying in quotes is taken from a well-known rule of logic formulated in the Talmud. He uses it here to argue that what is needed by individual Jews is needed by the people as a whole. Solomon Maimon (1754-1885) was a typical example of a deep Jewish thinker who had to acquire elementary knowledge when he was already renowned. He adopted the name Maimon because of his admiration for Maimonides.

We must, however, realise from the outset that this reconcentration of our scattered spiritual energies is not an easy matter, to be taken in our stride. The establishment of a home of refuge for Jewish culture perhaps demands preparation no less elaborate, and resources no less ample, than does the establishment of a home of refuge for persecuted Jews; and besides preparing for the future, we have a great deal of current work to do. We are all familiar with the division of Zionist opinion on the question of the attitude of Zionism to the current problems of the diaspora. My own opinion is that efforts to improve the economic and political position of Jewish communities in the diaspora are not strictly within the province of Zionism. Work of that kind of course has to be done, and it is useful as a means of obtaining some temporary alleviation of the position, however slight.

It has an undoubted claim on all those who are in a position to help. But life in exile, at its best, will always remain life in exile—that is to say, the opposite of that free national life which is the object of the Zionist movement; and a single movement cannot concern itself with two opposites. The case of cultural work is not analogous. The creative Jewish genius remains the same throughout history, and it has continued to function and to be true to itself even in the dispersion. Every spark of it that breaks away and floats into the outside world is an irreparable loss to our nation. To regain these lost sparks, to keep them at home for the benefit of our own culture, is essentially Zionist work, because by adding immediately to our spiritual assets it helps to pave the way for the larger cultural enterprise on which we shall embark after the establishment of the centre in Palestine, when the work of these returned wanderers will serve as the starting point for an advance into higher realms of achievement.

Should Zionism concern itself only with Palestine or should it be interested also in the affairs of the Jewish communities outside Palestine and thus become a kind of Jewish world government? Ahad Ha-Am thinks that such work in the political sphere is absurd. A movement such as Zionism which, basically, holds that life outside Palestine can only be a second-best for Jews, cannot at the same time take positive steps to be concerned with the fate of Jews in the diaspora. Of course, Ahad Ha-Am is not heartless and he urges anyone who can help Jews in the diaspora to do so, but this cannot possibly be the aim of Zionism as a movement. In that case should Zionists be interested in furthering Jewish culture in the diaspora? Ahad Ha-Am answers yes. His distinction is that Jewish social and political life outside Palestine is not ideally Jewish from the Zionist point of view. But Jewish culture is such wherever it is found. It is part of the Jewish heritage to be reclaimed for the Jewish people. Because of such arguments Ahad Ha-Am was considered the founder of cultural Zionism.

CHAPTER 20

A State is born

An affirmation of freedom.

All the discussions and debates regarding the nature of Jewish peoplehood obviously received a completely new turn with the establishment of the State of Israel and many of them became academic. The following is the declaration of the establishment of the State of Israel signed by Mr. David Ben-Gurion and members of the provisional council of state and members of the provisional government.

ERETZ-ISRAEL was the birthplace of the Jewish people. Here their spiritual, religious and political identity was shaped. Here they first attained to statehood, created cultural values of national and universal significance and gave to the world the eternal Book of Books.

After being forcibly exiled from their land, the people kept faith with it throughout their Dispersion and never ceased to pray and hope for their return to it and for the restoration in it of their political freedom.

Impelled by this historic and traditional attachment, Jews strove in every successive generation to re-establish themselves in their ancient homeland. In recent decades they returned in their masses. Pioneers, *ma'apilim* and defenders, they made deserts bloom, revived the Hebrew language, built villages and towns, and created a thriving community, controlling its own economy and culture, loving peace but knowing how to defend itself, bringing the blessings of progress to all

the country's inhabitants, and aspiring toward independent nation-hood.

In the year 5657 (1897), at the summons of the spiritual father of the Jewish State, Theodor Herzl, the First Zionist Congress convened and proclaimed the right of the Jewish people to national rebirth in its own country.

This right was recognized in the Balfour Declaration of the 2nd November, 1917, and reaffirmed in the Mandate of the League of Nations which, in particular, gave international sanctions to the historic connection between the Jewish people and Eretz-Israel and to the right of the Jewish people to rebuild its National Home.

The catastrophe which recently befell the Jewish people—the massacre of millions of Jews in Europe—was another clear demonstration of the urgency of solving the problem of its homelessness by re-establishing in Eretz-Israel the Jewish State, which would open the gates of the homeland wide to every Jew and confer upon the Jewish people the status of a fully-privileged member of the comity of nations.

Survivors of the Nazi Holocaust in Europe, as well as Jews from other parts of the world, continued to migrate to Eretz-Israel, undaunted by difficulties, restrictions and dangers, and never ceased to assert their right to a life of dignity, freedom and honest toil in their national homeland.

In the Second World War, the Jewish community of this country contributed its full share to the struggle of the freedom-and peace-loving nations against the forces of Nazi wickedness and, by the blood of its soldiers and its war effort, gained the right to be reckoned among the peoples who founded the United Nations.

On the 29th November, 1947, the United Nations General Assembly passed a resolution calling for the establishment of a Jewish State in Eretz-Israel; the General Assembly required the inhabitants of Eretz-Israel to take such steps as were necessary on their part for the implementation of that resolution. This recognition by the United Nations of the right of the Jewish people to establish their State is irrevocable.

This right is the natural right of the Jewish people to be masters of their own fate, like all other nations, in their own sovereign State.

ACCORDINGLY WE, MEMBERS OF THE PEOPLE'S COUNCIL, REPRESENTATIVES OF THE JEWISH COMMUNITY OF ERETZ-ISRAEL AND OF THE ZIONIST MOVEMENT, ARE HERE ASSEMBLED ON THE DAY OF THE TERMINATION OF THE BRITISH MANDATE OVER ERETZ-ISRAEL AND, BY VIRTUE OF OUR NATURAL AND HISTORIC RIGHT AND ON THE STRENGTH OF THE RESOLUTION OF THE UNITED NATIONS GENERAL ASSEMBLY, HEREBY DECLARE THE ESTABLISHMENT OF A JEWISH STATE IN ERETZ-ISRAEL, TO BE KNOWN AS THE STATE OF ISRAEL.

WE DECLARE that, with effect from the moment of the termination of the Mandate, being tonight, the eve of Sabbath, the 6th Iyar, 5708 (15th May, 1948), until the establishment of the elected, regular authorities of the State in accordance with the Constitution which shall be adopted by the Elected Constituent Assembly not later than the 1st October, 1948, the People's Council shall act as a Provisional Council of State, and its executive organ, the People's Administration, shall be the Provisional Government of the Jewish State, to be called "Israel."

THE STATE OF ISRAEL will be open for Jewish immigration and for the Ingathering of the Exiles; it will foster the development of the country for the benefit of all its inhabitants; it will be based on freedom, justice and peace as envisaged by the prophets of Israel; it will ensure complete equality of social and political rights to all its inhabitants irrespective of religion, race or sex; it will guarantee freedom of religion, conscience, language, education and culture; it will safeguard the Holy Places of all religions; and it will be faithful to the principles of the Charter of the United Nations.

THE STATE OF ISRAEL is prepared to cooperate with the agencies and representatives of the United Nations in implementing the resolution of the General Assembly of the 29th November, 1947, and will take steps to bring about the economic union of the whole of Eretz-Israel.

WE APPEAL to the United Nations to assist the Jewish people in the building-up of its State and to receive the State of Israel into the comity of nations.

WE APPEAL—in the very midst of the onslaught launched against us now for months—to the Arab inhabitants of the State of Israel to preserve peace and participate in the upbuilding of the State on the basis of full and equal citizenship and due representation in all its provisional and permanent institutions.

WE EXTEND our hand to all neighboring States and their peoples in an offer of peace and good neighborliness, and appeal to them to establish bonds of cooperation and mutual help with the sovereign Jewish people settled in its own land. The State of Israel is prepared to do its share in common effort for the advancement of the entire Middle East.

WE APPEAL to the Jewish people throughout the Diaspora to rally round the Jews of Eretz-Israel in the tasks of immigration and up-building and to stand by them in the great struggle for the realization of the age-old dream—the redemption of Israel.

PLACING OUR TRUST IN THE ALMIGHTY, WE AFFIX OUR SIGNATURES TO THIS PROCLAMATION AT THIS SESSION OF THE PROVISIONAL COUNCIL OF STATE, ON THE SOIL OF THE HOMELAND, IN THE CITY OF TEL-AVIV, ON THIS SABBATH EVE, THE 5th DAY OF IYAR, 5708 (14th MAY, 1948).

CHAPTER 21

The soul of Jewishness

What is special about the Jewish people.

*Nachman Krochmal (1785-1840), philosopher and historian, was one
of the first thinkers of modern times to consider the meaning of
Jewish peoplehood. The following is from the beginning of Chapter
8 of his* Moreh Nevukhe Ha-Zeman, *"The Guide for the Perplexed
of Our Time."*

The Eternal People and the Times Through Which It Passes

> **"For I the Lord change not;**
> **And ye, O sons of Jacob, are not consumed."**
> > **(Malachi 3:6)**

*Krochmal considers the role of Israel, the Jewish people, in the
modern world. His main thesis is that Israel is devoted to what he
calls "The Absolute Spirit"—God, Who is the Source of all spiritual
ideas. Other peoples also have spiritual values, of course, but Israel
is dedicated to the furtherance of the spiritual in its most absolute
and eternal form. Therefore Israel's work is never done. Some thinkers
used Krochmal's ideas to construct a theory of a special Jewish
mission to the world. Following this idea they argued that the Jewish
dispersion among the nations was not really exile at all but God's
means of enabling the Jews to spread the truth among all mankind.*

*Krochmal's idea here is that Israel may have its "ups and downs"
but it will never disappear completely because it is wedded to the*

God-idea which is eternal. Hence the title of the chapter under discussion: "The Eternal People and the Times Through Which It Passes." These times include periods of decline as well as of growth, but Israel can never decline to the extent of vanishing completely from the human scene. Krochmal was particularly good at finding apt quotations from the classical Jewish sources for his views. Here he quotes the verse from Malachi as a chapter heading. Because God does not change, the Jews committed to Him "are not consumed"; they share in His eternity.

Every ancient people, in obedience to natural law, passes through three distinct stages from the time it becomes a nation until it passes away and vanishes from the scene.
1. First, there is a period of growth, when, as we have said, the nation gives birth to the spiritual values to which it is dedicated. During this period the nation prepares its values and its people become united in a common bond in order to realize its spiritual advancement and perfection. This is called the period of the nation's growth, the time when it becomes a nation.

Krochmal's understanding of the history of civilizations is as follows. Every nation has its national ideal, its special idea, which acts as a cohesive force. The Greeks, for example, became great through their pursuit of beauty and philosophy, the Romans through their cultivation of law and government. The particular idea or value of a nation is its "god" to which everything in the national life is subordinated. It is this ideal which welds the individuals of which the nation is composed into a group with common aims and enables them to function together as a nation. With the growth of its particular idea the nation assumes its national guise and becomes endowed with its specific national genius. Note that Krochmal's analysis, despite its religious tone, is a modern, philosophic one. His system of thought seems to follow that of Hegel, one of the most sophisticated and influential minds of the century.

2. Then there is the period of realization when all those ideas to which we have referred receive their fullest expression and the nation becomes great because of these, acquiring fame and glory for a long or short span. This is called the period of the nation's power and activity.

The second period is that of the nation's golden age. The specific values for which it stands have now grown to the fullest of which they are capable, the thinkers and poets of the nation are busy teaching them and the ordinary folk applying them. The fame of the nation is widespread and others admire it for its achievements.

3. However, just as every living thing contains within itself the cause of its own death and destruction so, too, during this second period of ascendancy the seeds are sown for the nation's loss and ultimate dissolution. These germs of destruction wax ever stronger to disconnect all the bonds of unity and to destroy every good custom and the nation's honor progressively decreases until it is utterly destroyed. This is called the period of dissolution and decline.

Every living thing, by virtue of being such, contains the seeds of its own ultimate destruction. Energy, for example, is being used up all the time, otherwise a living thing could not live, and this, in itself, is a kind of preparation for death. Similarly a nation has to have something to live for and this is provided, as Krochmal has said, by the specific value to which its life is devoted. During the first period this value or idea beckons the people onward. As they meet with success they are inspired to work for even greater successes. But once the second period has been reached, its very success means that already there is far less to strive for. It is correct that nothing succeeds like success but when the ultimate in success has been achieved only failure can follow. When a nation cannot go higher it must perforce begin to go down. Once the limit of achievement is reached, boredom sets in, the sense of purpose is lost, the common ties are dissolved and the nation, no longer having anything to live for as a nation, begins to lose its identity. Its specific ideas do not die but become the property of all mankind, the contribution of that nation to civilization, as Greek art and philosophy and Roman law and government now belong to all humanity. Once having made this contribution the nation itself no longer has any reason for existing as a specific group, no aim or purpose peculiar to itself to endow its national life with individual significance. This explains why the great civilizations of the past—Egyptian, Babylonian, Greek, Roman, etc.—all had their day and then declined.

This process is to be observed at work in all nations dedicated to *particular* **spiritual ideas. Because these are** *particular* **they are finite**

and hence doomed to eventual destruction. It is otherwise with regard to our nation. In relation to our material world and external environment we, too, are subject to the natural laws, to which we have referred, of growth and decay. Yet our Rabbis of blessed memory say: "When Israel was exiled to Babylon the Divine Presence went with them in exile. When Israel was exiled to Elam the Divine Presence went with them in exile." This means that the *general* spiritual idea that is within us acts as a shield to deliver us from the laws governing the transient. All this follows from what has been said earlier.

A nation wedded to a particular idea or ideas has, as its purpose for existing as a nation, a finite thing, an idea that by its nature is not unlimited. The pursuit of beauty, for example, cannot act as a permanent spur for national growth because although people can go on producing beautiful things eventually satiety sets in. People become tired of pursuing the same limited, albeit tremendous, idea. Since it is finite the people dedicated to it cannot be eternal. But Israel is dedicated to God. God is not one particular idea but the sum total of all that there is and hence His truth is inexhaustible. Man can never completely succeed in realizing this idea because the more one progresses the more there is to be achieved. God is Infinite and so there is no end to the challenge He provides and the effort He summons forth. The nation dedicated to God—Israel—therefore suffers decline as other nations do, but always rises again because its task is never finished. Notice how skillfully Krochmal applies the Rabbinic saying about the Divine Presence. God's Presence—the absolute spirit—always dwells with Israel and therefore even in exile they are imperishable. Notice, too, that Krochmal interprets the life of Israel in terms of national life. His is a most unusual synthesis of modern ideas of nationality and the life of the spirit. Neither alone would be meaningful to him.

Krochmal goes on in this chapter to trace through Jewish history the successive periods of growth, ascendancy and decline. It seems from his presentation that he believed that in his own day—the early nineteenth century—the Jews had just been through a period of decline and a new period of growth awaited them.

God may not be ignored

How far Jewish nationalism should go.

Rabbi Ignaz Maybaum (b. 1897), prominent Reform Rabbi and theologian, discusses in the following passage the scope of the nationalistic idea in Judaism and where, at times, it seems to conflict with greater Jewish values. The passage is from Maybaum's book The Faith of the Jewish Diaspora *(Vision Press Ltd., London, 1962, pages 145-148) and is in the form of a sermon which Maybaum preached in his synagogue in 1956. The Hebrew word* Shira *means "song of praise" and here refers specifically to the Song of Moses (Exodus, chapter 15). The title of the sermon quoted here is* National Anthems.

Tomorrow we read the *Shira*. *Shira* means song, but the proper interpretation would be 'The Song'. To the Jew no other song is comparable to the one which Moses sings: 'Sing ye to the Lord, for He hath triumphed gloriously: the horse and his rider hath He thrown into the sea' (Exodus 15,1). This song praises God who alone is King and who is the victorious King. Poets may sing of the victories of kings; the *Shira* sings of the victory of God. Poets may sing of the glories of the kingdoms and realms which human courage and splendid genius may establish for a span of time in history. The *Shira* sings of the eternal victory of God who alone is the Lord of history. In their national anthems the gentiles sing of the happiness of having their states; the

Shira sings of the birthright of the Jewish people to carry the yoke of the Kingdom of God.

With the establishment of the State of Israel, we Jews too have our national anthem. How will this change affect us? Honest thinking will be necessary to help the Jewish people to overcome the dilemma: *Shira* or national anthem? Today it is, in fact, not merely the 'either-or' of *Shira* or national anthem. Today there are three possibilities: the national anthems of the gentiles, the Jewish national anthem and the *Shira*. May God help us to find the right solution on which so much depends.

Maybaum deals here with the whole problem of Jewish nationalism from the religious point of view. From Biblical times onward Jews preferred to sing the praises of God rather than the praises of their nation. But now that there is a State of Israel it cannot differ in many ways from other States and, among other things, it also has a national anthem. This serves to pinpoint the problem. The words of the Jewish national anthem—the Hatikvah—do not refer to God but to the Jew's longing for restoration in his ancient homeland. But Maybaum and other religious thinkers would deem it the greatest tragedy if, as a result of the new conditions, Jews began to think less of God's deliverances and more of their people's might and prowess. This is the problem to which Maybaum addresses himself.

When I sing 'God save the Queen' I do it both with happiness and with sincerity. I am a Jew of many countries. My English passport is the fourth I hold. My first one was an Hungarian, my second an Austrian, my third a German. I am a Jew driven out from Germany where I spent the formative years of my life and where I settled down and where I thought I would live all my life. I became a refugee, driven out from the country which I had learned to love. All this explains my happiness and sincerity when singing: God Save the Queen, and I feel I am obeying the solemn commandment of Jeremiah who wrote to the Jewish people in Babylon: 'And seek the peace of the city whither I have caused you to be carried away captives, and pray unto the Lord for it: for in the peace thereof shall ye have peace' (29,7).

Jews have always been taught, from the time of Jeremiah, to look upon themselves as citizens of the lands in which they were given a

*home and to work and pray for the success of those countries. The
devout Jew, therefore, will be happy to sing the English or American
national anthem and so on. But now that Israel exists there is
another national anthem with meaning for the Jew, the Hatikvah.*

When I sing the *Hatikvah*, the Jewish national anthem, I think of my
brethren in Israel. I pray for them with sincerity. I must stress this
sincerity because I hold no brief for the ideology which demands that
every Jew should settle in Israel. The sincerity of my prayer for Israel
is mixed with anxiety about the dangerous political situation in which
my brethren in Israel have to live. Singing the Jewish national anthem
I also give vent to my hope that the State of Israel will mean help to
the Jews of the backward countries of the Middle East. After this
heart-searching I realise that I cannot sing a national anthem, be it
'God Save the Queen', or the *Hatikvah,* in the natural happy way in
which the gentiles sing their national anthems. I ask myself, again and
again, what I have left out. What has my heart not given, that the heart
of the gentiles give in abundance when they sing *their* national
anthems.

*Some Zionists argue that the ideal is for every Jew eventually to
settle in Israel and that anyone who rejects this has no right to sing
the Hatikvah which, for them, means just this. Maybaum denies
that he is being insincere when he sings the Hatikvah even though
he does not subscribe to that ideology. He thinks of the Hatikvah as
a prayer for the success of the State of Israel and this is the hope of
Jews who do not necessarily wish to settle there themselves. But,
having defended the need for singing both national anthems,
Maybaum still finds himself with reservations.*

I think I have found the answer. The national anthem dates back to
the French Revolution, which was a messianic event. Its message was
liberty, equality and fraternity. The gentiles are no longer mere gentiles, pagan groups; they are Christian gentiles. As nations they speak
the benediction 'Thou hast chosen us, Thou hast given us a mission'.
This election does not make them the priestly nation which we Jews
aspire to be. The gentiles remain political nations, divided among
themselves into those who are leaders and those who are led. Whereas
Jewish election makes the Jew stand before his God without a mediator, the Christian gentiles have their mediator. Besides God who is the

King of all kings, as the *Shira* proclaims, the Christian gentiles say they possess incarnated in history that which they refuse to regard as passing history. Singing their national anthems, the Christian gentiles establish a new love at the side of God which is not the love commanded in the 'Hear O Israel: Thou shalt love the Lord thy God with all thy heart, with all thy soul and with all thy might.' In their national anthems the Christian gentiles awaken a love which they cherished with all their heart, with all their soul and with all their might, but which is no longer directed to God who is God and none besides Him. The national anthem is a Christian psalm, and full of national fervour and love, but nevertheless Christian. The Christian psalmist of the national anthem sings with his heart full of love; he expresses a love which embraces time as if it were eternity. Love always says: 'For ever'. But only God is eternal, God who is God and none besides Him. He is the God to whom the Jew alone turns, obeying the commandment: 'Thou shalt love the Lord thy God with all thy heart, with all thy soul and with all thy might.'

By a "messianic event" Maybaum means an event which is the culmination of centuries of human hopes and strivings and is, therefore, the "end" in the sense that what it celebrates will last forever. Maybaum believes that this belongs to the Christian doctrine of the Incarnation i.e. that Jesus is the Messiah and therefore an historical event become eternal. Judaism does not believe this. Now, argues Maybaum, the trouble with all national anthems (which arose as a result of Christian influence) is that they sing of the nation and its ideas as if they are the final aim and to which a man should give his total allegiance. But the Jew can only give this to God. While Maybaum is certainly right in arguing that a Jew can never worship his nation, only his God, it is questionable whether he is fair to Christians, many of whom would agree with him. There are no references, in fact, to Christianity in the national anthems.

The flag of the State of Israel is a noble flag, no less so than the Union Jack or the Old Glory. Jewish youth died for the blue and white flag with the *Magen David*. The greater number of men represented by the Union Jack or even more by the American flag has nothing to do with the nobility with which a flag is surrounded. That man is prepared to die for his flag, makes the flag a noble symbol. But just because the Jewish flag is as noble as the Union Jack and the American flag, just because the life of this present Jewish generation possesses the noble symbol of a flag, a symbol raised to such importance that we are prepared to die for it as our fathers died for their faith, we are aware that we may become what the Christian gentiles are. I do not say that this must be so. The Israeli patriot can remain a Jew just as we, singing 'God Save the Queen', shall remain Jews. But we suddenly realise when singing the *Hatikvah* we are singing the song of the gentiles, the song of love devoted not to the God of whom the *Shira* sings. We must, indeed, be careful. Only as long as we understand the *Shira*, the song of Moses, can we Jews sing a national anthem and yet be Jews worshipping the God of our fathers.

Love of one's people is a great thing and should not be made light of. It is "noble." But only God is to be worshipped, and care must always be taken that the nation does not become our object of worship. The worship of a State or a nation is a modern form of idolatry. It is only fair to record that many "gentile Christians" have also said this.

The above sermon was preached on Friday evening. Next morning a sermon about the relationship of the *Shira* and the national anthems was explained to the children on these lines: Manasseh ben Israel said to Cromwell: 'The Messiah cannot come until Jews are allowed to live in every country of the world'. Manasseh ben Israel's formula can be put in another way. The Messiah cannot come until Jews are able to sing the national anthems of the gentiles everywhere. The *Shira*, compared with a national anthem, can be called the national anthem of all mankind.

Manasseh ben Israel was the statesman who tried to persuade Oliver Cromwell three hundred years ago to re-admit the Jews into England. Cromwell was a believing Christian and he believed, too, in the coming of the Messiah. Manasseh told him that he ought to let the Jews live in England and that other nations should also admit the Jews, because until Jews were able to live everywhere the Messiah could not come. Maybaum gives this tale a fresh touch. When the peoples of the world sing only of their own nation and not of God there cannot be peace and happiness for all mankind and the Messianic Age cannot dawn. The Jew cannot sing that kind of national anthem. But once the nations learn to worship only God and as a result work for all mankind, then the Jew can join them. When that happens the Messianic Age will have dawned.

Citizens of the widest world

Jewish nationalism—its relevance to a wider view of life.

Rabbi Morris Joseph (1848-1930) was, from 1894, senior minister of the Reform congregation in London but previously served as an Orthodox Rabbi. His viewpoint is midway between Reform and Orthodoxy on many matters. In this passage from his book Judaism as Creed and Life *(Routledge & Kegan Paul Ltd., London, 1903, pages 167-172) Joseph discusses the meaning of the doctrine of the coming of the Messiah in the light of the thought prevalent in his day.*

The Jew, then, looks forward to a future of universal religion and righteousness. He pictures to himself a Golden Age; but, unlike the Pagan peoples of old, he places it in the future, not in the past. The world, he holds, is progressive; mankind is slowly but surely marching on to a happier time of faith and goodness, when men "shall not hurt nor destroy: for the earth shall be full of the knowledge of the Lord, as the waters cover the sea" (Isaiah 11:9). That time is called the time of the Messiah or the Messianic era. The great Prophets of Israel loved to dream and to speak of it. They would turn with joy from the contemplation of present woes, national and human, to the thought of an era of unbroken peace and happiness, lying far away in the unknown future. They would comfort themselves and their hearers, under the oppressive sense of widespread moral corruption, with visions of a time when men should "cast away their idols of silver and their idols

of gold" and serve God "with one consent" (Isaiah 2:20; Zephaniah 3:9). Some of their pictures of this Golden Age are doubtless allegorical, full of the imaginative glow that characterises the literature of the East. Thus Isaiah can see the wolf and the lamb, the leopard and the kid, dwelling peaceably together, and a little child leading them (Isaiah 11:6). It is an exquisite picture, but a highly poetic one, which we must not take too literally.

Joseph, like many other Jewish thinkers of his day, had a strong belief in human progress. Note how he thinks of the Golden Age as being realized because "mankind is slowly but surely marching on . . ." The events of this century—two global wars, the death camps, the atomic bomb—have made such a picture far too optimistic and unrealistic for many thinkers today. A number of the Rabbis, in fact, do not think of the Messianic Age as something which comes through human effort and progress but through God's intervention. Note, too, how Joseph ignores the "nationalistic" part of the Prophetic vision. In the verse he quotes from Isaiah 11:9 the Prophet actually says: "they shall not hurt nor destroy in all My holy mountain," words which Joseph omits.

Yet another point is to be borne in mind. Not all the Prophetic descriptions of coming joy refer to a remote future, or foreshadow a condition of world-wide happiness. Some relate exclusively to the Prophet's own time, and announce events affecting the destinies of Israel only. Many of these predictions, however, have been interpreted in a directly opposite sense. They have been regarded as foreshadowing the advent of a Messiah, of a man, that is to say, belonging to the House of David, and endowed with almost superhuman gifts of mind and character, who in an age yet to come is to lead Israel back to Palestine, and to inaugurate the reign of religion and righteousness on earth. But in reality what they announce is the coming of a sovereign like King Hezekiah, for example, who lived in the Prophet's own time, and whose rule brought much-needed peace and well-being to his sorely tried people (see e.g. Isaiah 9:6,7). Even the word "Messiah," as used in the Hebrew Bible, has not that half-supernatural significance which it has come to possess. It means only the "anointed one," and was applied to ordinary Israelitish kings like Saul, and David, and Zedekiah, and even to a foreign potentate like Cyrus (I Samuel 24:6; II Samuel 22:51; Lamentations 4:20; Isaiah 45:1). In like manner passages which, according to some interpreters, speak of a Golden Age yet to come, were meant only to portray in highly figurative language a happy state of things that began, and came to an end, long ago (see e.g. Isaiah 9:6,7; Hosea 2:18; Amos 9:14,15; Zechariah 10:9-17).

Forgetfulness of these facts has produced much mischief both within and without the pale of Judaism. History is full of Messiahs, of men who have given out sincerely or insincerely that they were Divinely chosen to resuscitate Israel's nationality, and to establish a heavenly kingdom on earth. Multitudes have believed in them, and have only discovered their mistake after much suffering. In Jewish history Bar Cochba in the second century, and Sabbatai Zebi in the seventeenth, and in Mohammedan history the Mahdi of the Soudan in our own day, are familiar examples of these false Messiahs.

Joseph comes out here strongly, like many other thinkers of his day, in favor of a Messianic Age rather than a personal Messiah. In addition to the reasons given here a number of Jewish thinkers preferred to speak of an Age rather than a person because of the importance of the latter in Christianity. Moreover, Joseph and those who thought like him wished to interpret the whole Messianic idea in universalistic terms i.e. the whole world will be united in that age and there will be no special significance to the holy land. Consequently, they tended to deny the whole notion of a personal redeemer leading the people back to their homeland, as Joseph, indeed, goes on to say.

It does not necessarily follow, however, that the belief in a Messiah or in the Restoration of the Jewish State is a delusion. There are millions of Jews, to say nothing of other religionists, who cling passionately to these beliefs. Among oppressed Jewish communities—and such communities still exist in these days—the belief in the national revival of Israel is a powerful solace and support under galling persecutions. Who would wilfully seal up the springs of so much blessing? Who would dare to tell these companies of sorrowing, trusting souls that their hope is vain, their faith a chimera? No one can say what the future has in store for us. It may possibly be God's will that Israel is once more to enjoy political independence, and be settled in his own land under his own rulers. It would be rash, moreover, to declare positively that even the Prophets could not have had this far-off event in their minds when they dreamed of the future. If, then, we meet with

Jews who proclaim themselves Zionists, who believe in the Return and in national revival, or who look forward to the advent of a personal Messiah, let no one venture to say dogmatically that they are wrong.

Note how cautious Joseph is in his attitude. In Joseph's day the national movement was gaining ground and, although he himself apparently does not share their particular mood, Joseph cannot bring himself to declare that they are definitely wrong.

But, on the other hand, the fact must be stated that there are many Jews, and their number is probably increasing, who do not and cannot believe in these things. They cannot believe in the Restoration of the Jewish State, for they hold that such an event would impede rather than promote the fulfilment of the great purpose for which Israel exists. The moral and religious education of the world, they maintain, can best be promoted by close contact between Jew and Gentile. Isolation, they argue, even though it be isolation in Palestine and accompanied by national independence, would mean failure for Israel's mission. Those who hold this opinion point in justification to the memorable saying of the Rabbins, already quoted, that the dispersion of the Jew over the earth was providentially designed as a means of winning the world for religious truth. They remind us also of that other Rabbinic utterance which declares that on the day the Temple fell the Messiah was born, the fulfilment of Israel's Messianic task begun. These persons cherish a strong faith in the future of Judaism; but for them it is a future marked by moral and religious triumphs, not by national glory. It is a spiritual empire, they affirm, that Israel is to win; and it can only be won by the Jew remaining a citizen of the world, and directly influencing the religious life of the world by his creed and his example. Moreover, in common with all Jews, they believe in a future not only for Israel, but for all mankind. They sincerely cherish the Prophetic faith in the advent of a Golden Age of universal peace and brotherly love. But they do not lay much stress upon details. Their picture of the earthly Paradise is purposely vague as is the Jewish dream of the heavenly Eden. A half-divine figure, who is to change the existing order of things by the waving of a magic wand, has no place in their thoughts. They believe implicitly in the Messianic Age; the idea of a Messianic Person they reject or ignore. They are inclined to agree with the old Rabbi who declared that

Israel had no longer a Messiah, seeing that he had enjoyed him in King Hezekiah, meaning thereby that the prophetic utterances which seem to foreshadow a "Prince of Peace" yet to come were fulfilled ages ago.

Joseph here advocates the mission of Israel idea as superior to that of national restoration. Actually his Rabbinic quotations are misleading. The Rabbis may have believed that Israel's dispersion was an act of Providence, but they clearly looked forward to an eventual restoration. The other saying simply means that the process of redemption was, as it were, set in motion from the very moment of destruction. Anyone who is familiar with Rabbinic literature knows that the Rabbis unanimously believed in a national restoration of the Jewish people to its ancient land. In addition, the following critique has been advanced against the mission of Israel idea: Is it not presumptuous for the Jews to declare that they are to be the teachers of mankind? Is it not better that they should first try to rebuild their own national home and then, by example, Judaism's teachings might well spread abroad?

Joseph puts the words "Prince of Peace" in quotes because this was the name given to Hezekiah but used of the Messiah by both Jews and by Christians who identified the figure of the Messiah with Jesus. Joseph uses the word "Rabbins," the old English word for "Rabbis." He means, of course, the Rabbis of the Talmud.

And surely we are no more at liberty to forbid these opinions than we are free to rebuke the minds that reject them. The question whether a Messiah is to be one of the figures of the Messianic Age, or whether Israel is to be a nation once more and the Temple in Jerusalem the religious centre of the whole world, is not a vital question. We can be equally good Jews whatever view we hold on these points. They are details on which freedom of thought can be tolerated without injury to the Faith.

But the same cannot be said of the Messianic Idea. That is one of the essentials of our creed, without which Judaism would have neither meaning nor life. If there is no Golden Age in store for the world, which the Jew is to bring nearer by his belief and his example, if Israel is never to behold the triumph of the great principles to which he has borne such pathetic witness, then Judaism is vain. To despair of that triumph is to confess that Judaism has no purpose to fulfil in

God's scheme. It is to deny its truth. If the dogma of the Divine Unity is the foundation of our religion, the Messianic Idea is its coping-stone.

Joseph makes an interesting distinction here between the belief in the dawn of the Messianic Age (which, for him, means a new era of peace and religious truth for all mankind) and the particular beliefs regarding the personal Messiah and the restoration. The belief itself is essential to Judaism. (Maimonides records belief in the Messiah as a basic principle of Judaism.) But the secondary beliefs are open, as it were.

In this respect Judaism is not too dogmatic, leaving a good deal of freedom to the individual human mind to decide which it prefers. But Joseph does not leave us in doubt as to which he himself prefers.

CHAPTER 24

The self and the folk

How far the individual Jew should become
subordinate to the Jewish people.

Rabbi S. Zevin, editor of the Encyclopedia Talmudit, *comments on the relationship of the individual to the group in his Introduction to Rabbi Abraham Chen's (1878-1958) Be-Malkhut Ha-Yahadut, "In the Kingdom of Judaism" (Jerusalem, 1959, pages 12-13). Rabbi Chen fought all his life for the rights of the individual. In his view it is the individual who has supreme significance. The group of which he is part exists for him, not the other way round.*

The generally accepted view is that the individual must give way to the group—not alone that the group takes precedence over the individual but that the group comes first even when it is a question of either-or. The individual is to be sacrificed for the good of the community— actually sacrificed, his blood and his flesh. Rabbi Chen's is a lone voice here. He argues that the principle according to which a distinction is made between one and more than one, can only apply with reference to means to an end, to instruments, to things, to that which *belongs* to someone. But independent entities, ends and not means, which are not things and do not belong to anyone else, these are ruled out from the beginning as having anything to do with mere numbers. A human being has no owner apart from himself. He is therefore his own and is, indeed, unique. One cannot make a total of two or three or more from human beings. Man exists for himself, not for something other than himself. He is an end and not a means to an end. He is unique, not one among many. Each human being has, as it were, no equal and there is none beside him. Man is created in God's image and shares His eternity. "Therefore one man was created: To teach you that whoever destroys a single human being it is as if he had destroyed a whole world." This is the version found in the Mishnah. In Avot de-Rabbi Natan the version is: "It is as if he had destroyed the whole six days of creation."

The group consists of a number of individuals and most people argue that it is right to sacrifice one for many. But Rabbi Chen cannot agree because he holds that the distinction between one and more than one cannot apply to human beings. For instance, if a man has to give away one of his chairs (or some other object he owns) in order to retain five other chairs, he is right to do so. Five chairs are better than one. But this is because chairs are things, they belong to someone, they do not exist in their own right but to be used. A human being, on the other hand, is a person not a thing (compare this with what Buber says earlier). His worth cannot be measured and, in any event, he exists for himself. No two human beings are alike and no one has the right to "measure" human beings, which one must do if one is to argue that five are superior to one. Note that Rabbi Zevin, interpreting Rabbi Chen, quotes "there is none beside him." This is originally a verse which speaks of God, and it is very bold to apply it to humans. But since man is created "in the image of God" this means that he, as an individual, is unique. This Mishnah deals with the story of Adam and Eve. One human pair become the ancestors of all men. This, says the Mishnah, is to teach you that a whole world can come from one human being and therefore anyone who destroys a human life destroys a whole world. Avot De-Rabbi Nathan is another Rabbinic work. Here it is said that Adam is created at the end of the six days of creation i.e. as the climax of the whole creation (see Genesis, chapter 1). Hence anyone who destroys a single life destroys a whole world. Rabbi Chen quotes these passages to stress that each human being is a whole world. The Mishnah says, "Therefore one man was created . . ." According to Rabbi Chen this is not incidental, as Rabbi Zevin goes on to say. This is why only one man was created at first. (The fact that most people, nowadays, do not take the Biblical story of Adam and Eve literally does not, of course, affect the fine idea contained in the ancient texts.)

Rabbi Chen stresses the word "therefore," on the face of it merely an auxiliary word. The Mishnah does not mean to say that this follows because man was created a single person but that this is *why* he was created a single person. The whole purpose of man's creation was to teach this fundamental principle. Man is unique. Consequently he is all. He is the whole world, the whole of the six days of creation. The view of the world—woe to such a world!—that the individual must yield to the group, which is made up of individuals like himself, has brought slaughter and the slaughterer into the world. It is this idea which has turned the whole world into one gigantic, legalized slaughter-house. For the distance between a prohibition of slaughter and permission to slaughter, between the right to kill and the prohibition of killing is immeasurable. But between *kosher* killing, as it were, and *non-kosher* killing there is not even the difference of two hairs-breadth. This outlook on life Rabbi Chen constantly substantiated. He expounded it with many variations and on numerous occasions from his first appearance on the literary scene, with his essay *Thou Shalt Not Kill,* until his dying day.

Rabbi Chen argues that an individual may never be sacrificed for his group. Consequently, no one, in his view, can ever justify such a killing, which would be murder. But once admit that sometimes an individual may be sacrificed for his group and the group will soon discover reasons for applying the principle in all kinds of circumstances. Then mass murder results. Rabbi Chen believes that so much horror and misery in the world is caused precisely by this—that there are always people ready to appeal to great ideals in order to sacrifice men to them. But the individual is the supreme value and no ideal is more important. This may lead to a complete pacifist view and maybe that is Rabbi Chen's attitude. On the other hand, he may have argued that it is permitted for a people to defend itself against attack but this should be seen as the defense of individuals. Rabbi Chen's real fear is that nationalistic and other ideologies may encourage wanton slaughter by an appeal to the sacrifice of the individual for the good of society. Rabbi Zevin has a rather clever pun here. According to the Rabbis the difference between the incision in the neck of an animal that is killed in the kosher way and one not so killed is the difference between the breadth of two hairs. Rabbi Zevin says that once one has legitimized killing, once it becomes kosher in some circumstances to kill a human being, then the way is wide open to wholesale

killing and the difference between the kosher *and the* non-kosher
is even less than the breadth of two hairs.

The time came when on this matter the whole world was on one side
and Abraham on the other—and yet he stuck to his guns. The State of
Israel was established! Rabbi Chen's poetic soul sang to Israel's redemption. Each Independence Day he used to deliver speeches on
the significance of Israel's freedom and its consequences for Jewish
life and he wrote a large number of essays on this theme. But even
the redemption could not be for him an ultimate aim for the sake of
which it is right for the individual to become a mere cog in the wheel.
He was fond of telling a story in illustration of this. I do not know
whether he ever put it into print but I myself heard him tell the story
on a number of occasions. It happened one Yom Kippur at the time
of Neilah that the Hasidic Master, Rabbi Levi Yitzhak of Berditchev,
led the congregation in prayer with special devotion. Rabbi Levi
Yitzhak refused to budge and the congregation awaited the outcome
with great fervor. But all of a sudden Rabbi Levi Yitzhak stopped his
devotions and rushed quickly through the remainder of the prayers.
After the fast this is what the Rabbi said. He said that he had tried hard
in that prayer to bring the Messiah for he saw that all hope was vanishing and the time had come. Only a little while longer and he was sure
that his aim of bringing the Messiah would be successful. But suddenly
the Rabbi realized that a certain Jew in the synagogue was very weak
from the long fast and would die if he was kept much longer in the
synagogue. So Levi Yitzhak completed his prayers quickly and the
whole plan of bringing the Messiah had to go by the board! I do not
know where he saw this tale or from whom he had heard it and I also
do not know whether any of us would agree to take the *motif* of the
tale for its practical application. But it is good that in our generation
one person should have stood firm in opposition to every one else to
proclaim the sanctity of man and of human life whether people listened to him or not. Such a one was Abraham.

*Rabbi Zevin refers to the story of Abraham who is described as "the
Hebrew." The Rabbis connect this word with the Hebrew word
ever, "a side" and say that Abraham stood on one side and all the
rest of the world on the other. Abraham was prepared to defy the
whole world in the name of his faith in One God. Rabbi Zevin*

applies this to Rabbi Abraham Chen. Rabbi Chen recognized the tremendous importance of the State of Israel but even this most lofty aim was not more important than the individual. Rabbi Levi Yitzhak of Berditchev was a famous Hasidic leader of the eighteenth century renowned for his pleading of the cause of the people of Israel, which makes the tale especially significant.

In the end of days

Belief in a personal Messiah.

*Steven S. Schwarzschild is Professor of Philosophy at Washington
University, St. Louis, and formerly Editor of Judaism. The following
extracts are from his article in Judaism (Spring, 1956) arguing for belief
in a personal Messiah.*

**If, then, we must discard the third main reason which the liberals of
the 19th century proffered for the abolition of the concept of the
personal Messiah, literally not one of their arguments has been found
to withstand critical examination. Their anti-nationalism has been repudiated by Jewish history; their anti-miraculousness has been refuted
by the necessities of their own position, not to speak of the views of
others; their optimism has been repudiated by general history. . . . In
short but brutal fact, their case against the personal Messiah crumbles
at the first touch.**

*The liberal Jews of the last century have unanimously rejected
belief in a personal Messiah (a person descended from the house of
King David, sent by God to redeem Israel and mankind) in favor of
the idea that a Messianic Age will dawn.*

*Schwarzschild cites three reasons the liberals felt obliged to reject
the traditional doctrine of a personal Messiah as follows: 1) The
idea was too nationalistic. It spoke of the prince who would come
to Israel, rather than the liberals' view of a better world which they
believed was just around the corner; 2) They believed that miracles*

had had their day and the idea of God sending a personal Messiah smacked too much of the miraculous; 3) They were optimistic about human progress and did not think it necessary for God to intervene directly. Mankind was moving automatically toward the Messianic Age.

Schwarzschild rejects each of these arguments. 1) Whether we like it or not the emergence of the State of Israel has made Jewish nationalism a reality; 2) Even the dawning of a Messianic Age can only be brought about by a miracle, so that there is little difference between God intervening directly and God working slowly through human history; 3) In the last century there were grounds for optimism about human history. But in our age, when such terrible events as the Holocaust have occurred, what grounds are there for this kind of optimism? In our age it is surely more reasonable to believe that the Messiah can only come through God's efforts, not through man's.

We could end the argument at this point. Religious tradition must always be regarded as valid until, and unless, invincible reasons are brought forth against it. The reasons militating against the traditional doctrine under consideration have been shown to be anything but invincible, and we may, therefore, with good and calm consciences return to the original position. Ours is not necessarily the task to prove the doctrine positively; to refute its refutation ought suffice. Nevertheless, without venturing to prove its tenability, there are a few hints which may be given toward the construction of the positive case.

Schwarzschild here says that once the arguments against the traditional view have been demolished there is no need to say more since the traditional view can now stand. However, he does try to undertake a defense of this view in itself.

The first is a mere technicality. The liberal prayerbooks of the last century have abounded, and still abound, with phrases which must, if they are to be intellectually acceptable, be interpreted very broadly by the Jews who use them. "The Torah of Moses" is as clear-cut an example as any, although there are many others. Do liberal Jews believe that "the" Torah was given to, by, or from Moses? As a matter of fact, the very ritual reading from the Torah has become a metaphoric act for most of them.

A very high percentage, certainly well over half, of everything read from it, if it is to be acceptable at all, must be homiletically decontaminated of its original historical, theological, moral, or social intent. And nonetheless these things are retained—re-interpreted but retained. Yet the phrase "Who brings a redeemer" cannot be so treated; it must be changed!? All that was required to bring the traditional text into conformity with liberal belief was the interchange of a single letter of the Hebrew alphabet, an *Heh* at the end for a *Vav* in the middle of the word. But this had to be done through a surgical operation on the prayerbook, when much more serious problems were solved with exegetical palliatives. We may assuredly draw two conclusions from this observation: 1. There was more to this than meets the eye; more fundamental interests were involved than those that were expressed; 2. A return to the original phrase is justified if only because it will violate no one's conscience; completely free exegesis will still be offered to anyone who wishes to take advantage of it.

In analyzing the views of Hermann Cohen, we pointed out the intimate connection between the belief in the personality of the Messiah and the belief in the personality of God. For him, as for the liberal mentality in general, the entire concept of personality as such was a terrible stumbling-block. As Kierkegaard and existentialism never tire of pointing out, the existence of the individual personality defies all the universal and theoretical laws of science as well as of idealism. They, therefore, try to dissolve it into general propositions. God as an idea, the Messiah as an age—these are entities with which theoretical reason can deal. The persons of God and of the Messiah, on the other hand, are hard, stubborn, even—as it were—empiric realities that defy classification. But then, so does every individual. And thus, the de-personalization process does not stop with God or the Messiah so far as liberalism was concerned.

A change was likewise introduced into the second benediction of the *Amidah*. "Praised be Thou, O Lord, who bringest to life the dead" seemed to be a liturgical formulation of the doctrine of resurrection, and this doctrine was regarded as outmoded as the reference to the personal Messiah. Do we not know that the body decomposes in the grave? Where would physical resurrection take place in the spiritual world of God? Does not the belief in the eternity of the body imply a vast over-emphasis on the material aspect of life? And so the modernistic arguments ran. Therefore, again the liturgical formulation was changed, and so remains to this day: "Praised be Thou, who hast implanted within us eternal life." In this manner, belief in the immortality of the soul was substituted for the concept of resurrection of the body.

The rejection of the belief in resurrection is closely connected with the rejection of the personal Messiah—not only because they both found expression at the very beginning of the *Amidah*. Ever since Ezekiel pictured the Messianic re-birth of Israel in terms of the famous revived bones, one of the traditional marks of the advent of the Messiah in Jewish thought has been the resurrection of the dead. "May the All-merciful make us worthy of the days of the Messiah and of the life of the world-to-come." And at the Conference of American Reform Rabbis in Philadelphia in 1869, the rejection of the one doctrine was immediately and logically followed up with the rejection of the other. Thus, the depersonalization process has gone one step further: God is not a person but an idea or a force; the Messiah is not a person but an age; and man is not a person but a universal reason confined in an individualizing and debasing body—a state of affairs fortunately remedied in the hereafter!

The Reformers changed the Hebrew words u-mevi goel, "who brings a redeemer" to u-mevi geulah, "who brings redemption" thus changing belief in a personal Messiah to belief in a Messianic Age. (Goel is formed by the letters gimmel, vav, alef, lammed, while geulah omits the vav and adds a heh). Schwarzschild argues that behind all these changes was really the idea that somehow it is more philosophical, more reasonable, more akin to our experience, to speak of God and religion in impersonal rather than in personal terms. An impersonal Messianic Age was more philosophically respectable than the coming of a personal Messiah. Hence the reference to Kierkegaard and existentialists, who reject this view. Everything can be reduced to scientific laws, but Kierkegaard and the others never tire of pointing out that the human being is free and, by virtue of this freedom, cannot be reduced to scientific laws, cannot be fitted into any tidy schemes, can always upset neat systems by behaving as he chooses. According to Schwarzschild's interpretation the liberals refused to recognize this and so they were suspicious of the idea of the personal God and the personal Messiah because it did not fit in with their neat schemes.

Herein also lies the most important reason for our time for a return to the personalism of the Messiah. Not only have we re-acknowledged the unitary character of the human person: if scientific conclusions have any bearing on this discussion, they tend to assert the indivisibility, even the indistinguishability of "body" and "soul." Martin Buber's philosophy of dialogue is premised on the recognition of persons, human and divine, as the carriers of life. The outlook of the Bible which deals with "the whole man" is re-asserting itself in the form of what is called "personalism." Baeck describes this outlook in these words: "It is particularly true of prophetic thinking that it is far removed from abstract descriptions and instead envisages the figure of a real human being with its views and deeds. The prophets speak less of a future time than of a future person. The ideal of the future becomes for them an ideal personality . . . The son of David is the future man. As a man of flesh and blood he makes real and vivid what the ideal man ought to be and will be." As Tillich puts it: "Ontology generalizes, while Biblical religion individualizes." And specifically with regard to the Messiah, the "liberal" Wiener puts the case clearly: "It is always the great miracle, the emergence into overpowering visibility of the deeds of God Himself, which characterize the days of the Messiah—the expression of the personal shaping of world-history by the personal God. For this reason so much emphasis is put on the personality of the Messiah . . . It is precisely in the belief in the Messiah that one can recognize the full vitality of a religiosity for which God is personality and His revelation the tangible guidance by means of miracle. One is inclined to say that at this point piety is most distantly removed from everything abstract, from conceptual ideology— and that it rather becomes faith in the true sense of the word, believing confidence in the revelation of concrete facts." We have learned from religious as well as non-religious existentialism, that all moral reality, as distinguished from nature or mathematics, is the reality of persons. Man, the person, is the *locus* of ethics, not ages, ideas, or forces. The messianic age is a utopia; the Messiah is a concrete, though future, reality.

The personal is, in fact, the most real thing there is, as the thinkers Schwarzschild quotes all acknowledge. We therefore do a disservice to Judaism if we give up the personal.

It might be here objected that, in fact, the doctrine of the personal

Messiah can de-personalize human life in that only one person—the
Messiah—is singled out and he is so extraordinary a person that his
being has little reference to the personality of normal human beings.

Let us consider one last objection which will be raised against this
view. It will be said again, as it has often been said in the past, that
reliance on the messianic fulfillment will lead to moral quietism and
passivism. If men expect a divine agent to bring about perfection, they
will sit back, relax their own efforts toward the good, and leave to
him the work they themselves ought to do. This has, indeed, often
happened.

Was it not a delegation of Orthodox rabbis of the *Aggudah* type who
requested the British mandatory governor not to withdraw his troops
since Zionism was human supererogation anyway, and the Messiah
was to come in 1999? But the drawing of an improper conclusion does
not mean that the doctrine ought be abolished. It ought rather be
protected against false interpreters.

Quietism is the doctrine that all human effort is futile and everything
must be left to God. This is not the Jewish attitude, which speaks of
man as a co-partner with God. Now it might be argued that the
doctrine of the personal Messiah sent by God will lead to quietism,
but this Schwarzschild denies.

"Perish all those who calculate the end," was the motto of the Talmudic rabbis who opposed the view that the messianic time was fixed
mechanically without regard to the human contribution to its hasten-
ing. They taught emphatically that the arrival of the Messiah was dependent upon man's actions: if they were good it would be sooner,
if evil—later. "God said: everything depends on you. Just as the rose
grows with its heart toward heaven, so do you repent before Me and
turn your hearts heavenward, and I will thereupon cause your redeemer to appear." There is even the view, which commends itself on
ethical grounds, that the Messiah will appear after the messianic state
has been established, leaving its attainment to humanity but guarantee-
ing its maintenance thereafter. Even Mendelssohn seems to have held
this view. The 19th century proto-Zionist, R. Hirsch Kalischer stipu-
lated the return to Zion as a pre-requisite, not consequence, of the
messianic advent. And even the man who was later to become one

of the foremost and most radical leaders of American Reform, Samuel Hirsch, in the days before he went to greater extremes, advanced this same thought. "It is up to us to turn to God, for the Messiah cannot come before we have become completely good . . . No, it is not the duty of the Messiah but that of the entire household of the vanguard against evil, the entire house of Jacob, to wage this battle on behalf of all the inhabitants of the world, and the root of Jesse cannot shoot forth out of its midst until it has fulfilled this duty and carried out its task."

From the quotes it follows that one can believe in the coming of a personal Messiah and yet still believe in the need for human effort as a prior condition.

Therefore, not only is it untrue that the doctrine of the personal Messiah must necessarily lead to quietism. On the contrary, it can help in suppressing the peculiar modern variant of pseudo-messianism. One of the most horrible and disastrous illusions to which modern men have fallen prey is that they have actually accomplished the messianic state. It is on the basis of this self-deception that our contemporary dictatorships have ruthlessly eliminated all dissent, for they maintain that dissent from perfection is, by definition, falsehood. Whereas in the Middle Ages pseudo-messianisms operated around a central, individual pseudo-messianic person, in our time it is characteristic of our collectivist and societally-minded frame of references that pseudo-messianisms take the form of national movements. More than ever, therefore, the absence of the person of the redeemer should constitute a constant warning against such blasphemous exaggerations. This warning is, furthermore, not without its applicability to the present Jewish world-situation. The messianic undercurrent in the history of modern Zionism has in turn led to the far-reaching secularization of "the messianic thought in Israel," as a result of which, as Leon Roth has pointed out, we no longer ask in the words of the Bible: "Who will recount the mighty deeds of God?" but rather in the words of the Israeli song: "Who will recount the mighty deeds of Israel?" What is even much more dangerous is the hazy notion floating through the minds of a not inconsiderable number of super-Zionists that the establishment of the State itself constitutes the messianic fulfillment. Here lies the road to certain disaster!

When Rabbi Kurt Wilhelm, formerly of Jerusalem and now chief-rabbi of Sweden, and this writer dared point out in a series of articles that Jewishly there is a vast difference between *yeshuah*, historical salvaging, and *ge'ulah*, redemption, an Israeli newspaper attacked us vehemently as new *Protestrabbiner!"* If this journalist had only been waiting for the Messiah!

Schwarzschild means that there is great danger in imagining that the Messianic Age has dawned and that therefore society is perfect when it is nothing of the kind. This tends to glorify whatever happens to be the political situation at the time, and evils and excesses can be justified. We need the reminder that the Messiah has not yet come and that we must still work for the perfect world under God.

The "Protest Rabbis" were the German Rabbis who rejected Zionism as contrary to the idea of universalism. Schwarzschild claims that he is not such a Rabbi but is only protesting against the identification of Zionism with the advent of the Messiah. It might also be said as a further point for discussion that Schwarzschild seems to imagine that the doctrine of the personal Messiah is the only traditional one and that it was only the nineteenth century liberals who rejected this. In fact, among the prophets, some seem to speak of a personal Messiah while others speak of a Messianic Age and at least one of the Talmudic Rabbis believed in the Messianic Age rather than in a personal Messiah. However, Schwarzschild is certainly correct in maintaining that the idea of a personal Messiah was the one generally held ever since the destruction of the Temple almost two thousand years ago.

Immortality and resurrection

What Judaism teaches about life after death.

I include the following from my book We Have Reason To Believe *(Vallentine, Mitchell & Co. Ltd., London, 1960, pages 118-124) because it is hard to find much in contemporary Jewish writing on the subject of the After-life. The first part of the chapter sketches the attitudes of the rabbis and the medieval thinkers as a background for the discussion of the problem today.*

The most striking difference between any modern interpretation of Judaism and the Judaism of Rabbinic and Mediaeval times is the shift in emphasis from an other-wordly to a this-wordly approach to the religious life. Even a cursory inspection of the traditional Jewish classics from the Talmud to Maimonides in the middle ages and to Moses Hayyim Luzzatto (1707-1746) on the threshold of the Emancipation, reveals the persistence of the doctrine of 'Olam Haba' (the 'World to Come') in the traditional scheme of Jewish theology.

To deal first with the Talmudic Rabbis, one need not be a particularly erudite rabbinic scholar to observe the strong other-wordly element in rabbinic theology. It is easy to be misled by such sayings as that a man will be obliged to give an account before the Judgment Seat of God for every legitimate pleasure he denies himself, for while it is true that many of the Rabbis were opposed to asceticism (though it must be said that in the wide range of rabbinic religious expression there is room for ascetic tendencies too) this did not prevent them teaching, as, indeed, is implied in this very saying, that this life is a preparation for the After-life. There is no basic incompatibility between the frank acceptance of this world and its pleasures as God-given and the conviction that what a man does with his earthly life is of eternal significance. 'This world is compared to the eve of the Sabbath, the next world to the Sabbath. Only he who toils on the eve of the Sabbath has food to eat on the Sabbath day'. 'This world may be compared to the land and the world to come to the sea. If a man lay not up provisions while on land, what will he eat when at sea'? 'This world is like a vestibule before the world to come. Prepare thyself in the vestibule that thou mayest enter the hall'. These sayings are entirely typical of the rabbinic outlook. Both the Rabbis and Josephus record that the Sadducees rejected the belief in an After-life but the Rabbis, the spiritual heirs of the Pharisees, inherited their beliefs so that such sayings as the above are never contested by any of the Rabbis. All the Rabbis share the belief in the immortality of the soul, it is the background to all they thought and taught. When the *Targum,* the official Aramaic paraphrase of the Bible, interprets the verse: 'Ye shall therefore keep my statutes and my judgments; which if a man do, he shall live in them . . .' to mean 'live in them in life eternal', it was but echoing a commonplace of the rabbinic teaching. One whole chapter of the Talmudic tractate Sanhedrin, deals almost entirely with the subject of the After-life and those who attain it. The Soncino translation in English can be consulted with profit for an account of the fascinating rabbinic views and speculations on *Olam Haba'*. The translator quotes with approval George F. Moore to the effect that although there are many speculations on the After-life in the Talmudic literature 'any attempt to systemise the Jewish notions of the hereafter imposes upon them an order and consistency which does not exist in them'.

During the Middle Ages, belief in the immortality of the soul continued to be held without dissenting voice. Typical of the 'great mediaeval thinkers is Maimonides, who treats this belief as a cardinal principle of Judaism and speaks disparagingly of those who entertain materialistic conceptions of the Life to Come. 'The good reserved for the righteous is life in the world to come, a life which is immortal, a good without evil. Thus it is written in the Torah: 'That it may be well with thee and that thou mayest prolong thy days'; the traditional interpretation of which is as follows: "that it may be well with thee," in a world which is altogether good; "that thou mayest prolong thy days" in a world which is unending, that is, the world to come . . .'

'In the world to come there is nothing corporeal and no material substance; there are only souls of the righteous without bodies, like the ministering angels. And since in that world there are no bodies, there is neither eating nor drinking, nor aught that human beings need on earth. None of the conditions occur there which are incidental to physical bodies in this world, such as sitting, standing, sleep, death, grief and merriment. So the ancient sages said: "In the life hereafter there is no eating, no drinking, and no marriage, but the righteous sit with their crowns on their heads and enjoy the radiance of the Divine Presence". This passage clearly indicates that as there is no eating or drinking there, there is no physical body hereafter. The phrase "the righteous sit" is allegorical and means that the souls of the righteous exist there without labour or fatigue. The phrase "their crowns on their heads" refers to the knowledge they have acquired and by virtue of which they attained life in the world to come . . . And what is the meaning of the Sages' statement: "they enjoy the radiance of the Divine Presence"? It means that the righteous attain to a knowledge and realisation of the truth concerning God to which they had not attained while they were in the murky and lowly body'.

Moses Hayyim Luzzatto was one of the most colourful personalities in the history of Jewish saintliness. Poet, kabbalist and moralist, he compiled his *Path of the Upright* as a guide to holy living. This work is still studied assiduously by pious Jews striving for self-improvement. The following, from the introduction to the *Path of the Upright,* is indicative of the other-worldly orientation of Luzzatto and his milieu. 'It is fundamentally necessary both for saintliness and for the perfect worship of God to realise clearly what constitutes man's duty in this world, and what goal is worthy of his endeavours throughout all the days of his life.

'Our Sages have taught us that man was created only to find delight in the Lord, and to bask in the radiance of His Presence. But the real place of such happiness is the world to come, which has been created for that very purpose. The present world is a path to that goal. "This world", said our Sages, "is like a vestibule before the world to come". Therefore, has God, blessed be His name, given us the *Mitzvoth*. For this world is the only place where the *Mitzvoth* can be observed. Man is put here in order to earn with the means at his command the place that has been prepared for him in the world to come. In the words of our Sages, "This day is intended for the observance of the *Mitzvoth;* the morrow for the enjoyment of the reward earned by means of them". No reasonable person can believe that the purpose for which man was created is attainable in this world, for what is man's life in this world? Who is really happy here and who content? "The number of our years is threescore years and ten, or even by reason of strength fourscore years, yet is their pride but travail and vanity", because of the suffering, the sickness, the pain and vexations which man has to endure, and finally death. Hardly one in a thousand finds that the world yields him true pleasure and contentment. And even that one, though he live a hundred years, passes away and is as though he had never been.'

'Moreover, if the purpose for which man was created is attainable in this world, why was he imbued with a soul which belongs to an order of existence higher than that of the angels, especially since the soul cannot enjoy any of the worldly pleasures? In commenting on the verse: "Neither is the soul filled", our Sages add, "The soul may be compared to a princess who is married to a commoner. The most precious gifts that the husband brings to his princess fail to thrill her. Likewise if thou wert to offer the soul all the pleasures of the world, she would remain indifferent to them, because she belongs to a higher order of existence".'

The evidence of these representative quotations—and they could quite easily be multiplied—is conclusive. The mediaeval Jew, like his Christian and Muslim counterpart, looked upon himself as a sojourner here on earth with his real home in heaven. Even in the twentieth century this attitude persisted. It is said that an American millionaire visited the Haphetz Hayyim and was astonished to observe the saint, whose fame had spread all over the Jewish world, living in great frugality. All that his room contained was a bare wooden table and a couple of chairs. 'Where is your furniture, Rabbi?' his guest asked the Haphetz Hayyim. 'And where is your furniture?' the sage asked him. 'My furniture! Why, Rabbi, what do you mean? I am only a visitor. My home is not here'. 'I too am only a visitor and my home is not here'! But in modern Jewish life, and even in modern Jewish religious teaching and preaching, there is an abrupt departure from the whole of the other-worldly conception. Judging by published sermons in English, references to the After-life are not very popular, to say the least, in present-day pulpit oratory.

We need not look far to account for the change. From the time of the French Revolution and the resulting Emancipation of the Jew, the Jewish people faced a problem of adjustment the like of which it had never encountered in its long history. When the walls of the Ghetto fell, Jews had to learn how to live as Jews in Western Society, how to preserve all that was of value in their tradition while participating to the full in the life of those States which had granted them equal civil rights with the rest of the population. Small wonder then that Jewish religious thinkers should have been preoccupied with such matters as Faith and Reason, Universalism and Particularism, Orthodoxy and Reform; all of them problems with immediate bearing on their practical life. The fate and prospects of the Jew in the realm of Eternity was naturally enough overlooked in the urgent struggle to enable Jews to live as good Jews in the world of Time. And no sooner had the bubble of Emancipation been rudely pricked than the beckoning dream of national revival came to the fore. Once again the best of Jewish thinkers busied themselves with immediate concrete problems. Ahad Ha-Am and Bialik preached the doctrine of the immortal soul of the people of Israel, urging Jews to make this the object of their striving. In an atmosphere in which the individual Jew who is at all idealistic works for the future of his people, he tends to forget, or, at least, to minimise, the importance of his own personal survival in a future existence.

Side by side with this Jews shared the general decline in belief in the hereafter typical of the past hundred years. The revolt against nineteenth century indifference to shocking social conditions here on earth because of the promise of future bliss, the widening horizons of Science, demonstrating for the first time the impossibility of a Heaven literally above us and a Hell gaping beneath our feet, the Religion versus Science controversy, materialist philosophy, all contributed to the rejection of belief in an After-life. Tennyson's tentative longings in his "In Memoriam'; the amazing popularity of Fitzgerald's Omar Khayyam; Marx and Lenin castigating religion as the 'opium of the people'; Shaw ridiculing a harp-playing Heaven and a coal-cellar Hell; these are all typical of Victorian and pre-1914 scepticism.

Among non-Jewish religious thinkers, this century has witnessed a reaction in favour of the other-worldly approach. The Great War and its aftermath of suffering, the horrors of Nazism and the concentration camps, the second Global War, the Atom Bomb and the threat of total annihilation have rudely shattered the facile belief that mankind will automatically progress to ever greater heights. No one can shirk today the issues raised by the revelation of man's depravity. So that Christian thinkers in particular are bent on reaffirming the importance of the belief in Immortality for a satisfactory religious outlook. Judaism alone, faced with the many problems raised by the emergence of the State of Israel and given new strength by its exhilarating potentialities, is unlikely to be affected by this reaction in the immediate future. Until the State of Israel is firmly established both materially and spiritually, Jewish thinkers are bound to be pre-eminently concerned with this life and its problems. And who can deny that there is something sublime in the persistent refusal of Jews to turn their back on life, to refuse to give up the struggle to establish the Kingdom of Heaven on earth? But sooner or later, the doctrine of the After-life, so inextricably woven into the fabric of Judaism, must come into its own. No really spiritual interpretation of Judaism is possible without it. The Hamlet of Judaism, if it is to be staged effectively, must not alone include the princely hero, the ghost too must not be omitted.

Is the belief in an After-life a worthy one? It has often been held suspect as pandering to our grasping instincts. It is suggested that it is ignoble for a man who does good to desire reward for so doing, that the whole notion is nothing more than an attempt at storing up good deeds in a spiritual bank upon which the calculatingly virtuous may draw. The believer, so the argument runs, denies himself certain immediate pleasures in the anticipation of more intense delights later on, much as a man may give up smoking for a time in order to save up to buy a car or a television set. But the delights of Heaven as interpreted by Judaism's greatest sons (we have noted above the views of Maimonides) are *spiritual*. C. S. Lewis has well said: 'Again, we are afraid that heaven is a bribe, and that if we make it our goal we shall no longer be disinterested. It is not so. Heaven offers nothing that a mercenary soul can desire. It is safe to tell the pure in heart that they shall see God, for only the pure in heart want to. There are rewards that do not sully motives. A man's love for a woman is not mercenary because he wants to marry her, nor his love for poetry mercenary because he wants to read it, nor his love of exercise less disinterested because he wants to run and leap and walk. Love, by definition, seeks to enjoy its object'. And it must not be forgotten that the person who believes in the After-life generally desires it not for himself alone but for others too. If it is virtuous to want human happiness to be increased here on earth why should it be considered ignoble to desire an increase of eternal happiness? Furthermore, without dwelling overmuch on theological niceties, if God created man for man's good—and this is the only reasonable conclusion to be drawn from belief in a benevolent, omniscient Creator Who can have lacked nothing before man's creation—then man, if he does not find complete happiness and fulfilment here on earth must find it in Heaven. Part of the saintly man's yearning for eternal life is a longing for God's justice to be vindicated.

In spite of what has been said, Judaism could teach a higher form of worship from which all thought of personal gain—even spiritual gain—is absent. 'Be not like servants who minister to their master upon the condition of receiving a reward; but be like servants who minister to their master without the condition of receiving a reward', is the saying of one of the earliest teachers of the Mishnah. An ancient version of this saying reads 'but be like servants who minister to their master on the *condition of not receiving a reward' (al menath shelo* instead of *shelo al menath).* The Hasidic teacher, Schneor Zalman of Ladi, was once overheard saying to himself: 'I desire not Thy Paradise, I desire not Thy Eden, but Thee alone'.

The bitterest complaint against the doctrine of the hereafter is that by directing men's minds heavenwards it diverts them from contemplating social evils and encourages them to tolerate bad social conditions. By it the rich are made complacent and the poor acquiescent. It is not within our purview to consider how far this accusation is justified with regard to other faiths but it is certainly not true of any widely held version of Judaism. In the Hebrew Scriptures the emphasis is so much on justice and righteousness in human affairs here on earth that, as we have been, the Sadducees could accept the Bible as the word of God and yet reject the belief in the hereafter. The idea that the poor can be safely neglected because God will compensate them for their sufferings in the hereafter has always been repugnant to the healthy Jewish religious conscience. Permeated as it is with the doctrine of the After-life, the Talmud meticulously surveys the social obligations of the Jew. The Talmudic regulations about such things as Communal taxation, poor relief, care for the sick and infirm, and education of the young show that the Rabbis were possessed of a social conscience far in advance of their time.

It would be futile to speculate on the nature of the After-life; Maimonides rightly says that when we discuss this subject we are like blind men trying to understand the nature of light. 'Know that just as a blind man can form no idea of colours nor a deaf man comprehend sounds, so bodies cannot comprehend the delights of the soul. And even as fish do not know the element fire because they exist ever in its opposite, so are the delights of the world of the spirit unknown to this world of flesh. Indeed we have no pleasure in any way except what is bodily. Anything else is non-existent for us: we do not discern it, neither do we grasp it at first thought, but only after deep contemplation. And truly this must necessarily be the case. For we live in a material world, and the only pleasure we can comprehend must be material. But the delights of the spirit are everlasting and uninterrupted, and there is no resemblance in any possible way between spiritual and bodily enjoyments. We are not sanctioned either by the *Torah* or by the divine philosophers to assert that the angels, the stars, and the spheres enjoy no delights. In truth they have exceeding great delight in respect of what they comprehend of the Creator (glorified be He!). This to them is an everlasting felicity without a break. They have no bodily pleasures, neither do they comprehend them, because they have no senses like ours enabling them to have our sense experiences. And so it will be with us too when after death the worthy from among us will reach that exalted stage'. Judaism knows too of cruder conceptions but it is safe to say that no representative Jewish theologian has ever countenanced anything like the sensual 'lemonade and dark-eyed houris' sort of Heaven. We are commanded to fast on Yom Kippur, says the Zohar, to teach that the pleasures of Heaven are non-material. Many of the Rabbis, with their devotion to Torah study, believed that Heaven can best be described as the 'Academy on High', in which God himself teaches the righteous His Torah. They believed too that humans can experience a foretaste of heavenly bliss in the delights of the Sabbath of which they spoke as *'Olam Haba* in miniature'.

The mystics in particular have taught that *eternal* life is quite different from endless duration in Time. Eternity is outside Space and Time. Strictly speaking we err when we speak of Heaven as the *Hereafter* or the *After-life* as if it were an extension of life in Time. The world of Eternity is not in Time at all; it is the world of Truth, the eternal *Now*, the world of Ultimate Reality. Indeed, in this view we ought not to speak of Heaven as a *place* but as a *state* of the soul; we ought rather to speak of 'becoming' Heaven (though even here human language prevents us from escaping from the categories of Time) than of 'going' to Heaven.

> I sent my Soul through the Invisible,
> Some letter of that After-life to spell:
> And by and by my soul returned to me
> And answered 'I Myself am Heaven and Hell'.

The mystics expound too the interesting doctrine of what they call 'bread of shame'—*nahama dekesupha*. If, they argue, God created man so that he inherits eternal life what is the purpose of the probationary period here on earth? Why could God not have created man in Heaven? Their answer is that there is a divine spark in man which refuses to be satisfied with undeserved good; a proud individuality and independence which causes him to reject spiritual benefits he has not earned, in the same way that a man here on earth prefers to work for his living than to eat 'bread of shame'. God, in other words, wants man to share in His Goodness by freely choosing the good—we must, indeed, go further and say that this freedom of choice is of the essence of the good. Eternal bliss is not to be understood so much as 'reward' for virtuous living. The pursuit of the good here on earth is itself the creation by man of his heavenly bliss.

And, be it noted, Heaven is frequently spoken of in the Jewish sources as a state of activity, of continuous progress in the knowledge and the love of God. 'The best definition of Hell' said Shaw, 'is a perpetual holiday'. The Rabbis anticipated him when they taught that the scholars have no rest either in this world or in the world to come. Rabbi Jonathan Eibeshütz (1690-1764) was a true disciple of theirs when he described the ancient legend about the righteous in Heaven dancing round God in a circle and pointing to Him and singing: 'This is my God and I will glorify Him', as a poetic way of depicting the life of Heaven as an ever-increasing knowledge of God. The metaphor of the circle is used, this author suggests, because the circle is finite but unbounded. The finite human mind will receive unbounded revelations of God's truth.

The strongest argument against the possibility of life beyond the grave is that the mind to all intents and purposes appears to be absolutely dependent on the brain. When the human brain is injured the human mind is affected, when the former decays the latter degenerates with it. How then, it is argued, can the mind live on after the body is no more? But the fact that the mind is dependent on the brain may only mean that it uses the brain as an *instrument*. The analogy of electricity is helpful here. Electric force can only be harnessed and used by the machinery we possess for this purpose but the force itself is quite independent of this machinery. It is not impossible that while in this life mind is dependent on the physical brain in the After-life it may not be so dependent.

H. E. Fosdick, who develops the above argument and whose statement of the religious view is altogether admirable, finely says: 'If a man is riding in his limousine, he is dependent on the windows for his impression of the outside world. If the glass is covered by curtains or besmeared with mud, he cannot see. All that happens to the windows affects his power either to receive impressions from without or to signal to his friends. Yet the man is not thereby proved to be the glass, nor is it clear that he may not some day leave his limousine and see all the better because the old mediums are now discarded. A man's dependence on his instruments can never be used to prove that he is his instruments or is created by them'.

In dealing with this subject a word must be said about the Jewish doctrine of Hell. It cannot be denied that there are to be found harrowing descriptions of 'life' in Hell in the Jewish writings of the Middle Ages as well as in the writings of the Church. Although the nobler thinkers speak not of physical pain but of the tormenting deprivation of the Divine Goodness, it is difficult to reconcile God's benevolence with His condemnation of any soul to eternal torment, even of a spiritual nature. Certain it is that, on the whole, Judaism does not know of the doctrine of *eternal* punishment. And certain too that the doctrine of Hell is not a dominant one in Judaism. One hears no preaching of Hell-fire in the Jewish pulpit and it is difficult to imagine a Jewish Rabbi in the last century saying, as Cardinal Newman did, that it were better for the earth and all that is in it to perish rather than that one soul should commit a single venial sin!

To sum up. As in so many other spheres Judaism steers a middle course, rejecting both extreme other-worldliness and non-attachment and hedonistic indifference to or atheistic denial of the After-life. It is, indeed, possible for a religion to be both this-worldly and other-worldly for, viewed from the aspect of Eternity, this world and the world to come are one. Eternity embraces the world of Time and what man does in the world of Time becomes his possession for all Eternity. It is this interaction between the two worlds that is at the heart of the paradox expressed by the ancient Jewish teacher: 'Better is one hour of repentance and good works in this world than the whole life of the world to come; and better is one hour of bliss in the world to come than the whole life of this world'.

This chapter may fittingly conclude with a note found on the body of the American Jewish soldier Colonel David Marcus who created the Army of the State of Israel. He called it: 'The Ship' and this is what he wrote:

'I am standing upon the seashore. A ship at my side spreads her white sails to the morning breeze and starts for the blue ocean. She is an object of beauty and strength, and I stand and watch her until at length she is only a ribbon of white cloud just where the sea and sky come to mingle with each other. Then someone at my side says, "There! She's gone!" Gone where? Gone from my sight—that is all. She is just as large in mast and hull and spar as she was when she left my side, and just as able to bear her load of living freight—to the place of destination. Her diminished size is in me, not in her, and just at the moment when someone at my side says, "There! She's gone!" there are other voices ready to take up the glad shout, "There! She comes!" And that is Dying'.